Meal Planning

Plan Your Meals with Low Carb and Grain Free Recipes

Andrea Griffin and Josephine Ramsey

Copyright © 2013 Andrea Griffin and Josephine Ramsey
All rights reserved.

Table of Contents

INTRODUCTION 1

SECTION 1: LOW CARB DIET 7

CHAPTER 1: RISE AND SHINE WITH A FORTIFIED BREAKFAST 10
- Crunchy Maple Grape Nuts 10
- Healthy Honey Oat Cereal 12
- French Toast Strawberry Dippers 14
- Breakfast Egg Muffins 16
- Cinnamon Raisin Muffins 19
- Asparagus and Mushroom Omelet 21

CHAPTER 2: LUNCHTIME RECIPES FOR AFTERNOON ENERGY 23
- Eggs, Lox and Caramelized Onions on Bagel 23
- Low-Cal Greek Salad 29
- Spinach Salad with Chicken and Raspberry 31
- Lettuce Roll-Ups with Pumpkin Seed Pate 33

CHAPTER 3: GREAT DINNER SURPRISES 36
- Mushroom Laced Meatballs 36
- Sassy Cheese and Chicken Enchiladas 39
- Colorful Veggie Meatloaf 42
- Grilled Summer Kabobs 44
- Veggie Laced Macaroni and Cheese 46

CHAPTER 4: UNIQUE SIDE DISHES 49
- Fake Mashed Potatoes 49
- Simplistic Green Beans 51
- Dressy Cauliflower Casserole 53

CHAPTER 5: FULFILLMENT WITH DRINKS 55
- Pina Colada Smoothie 55
- Refreshing Fruit Shake 57
- Awesome Juice Spritzer 58
- Honey Dew Smoothie 59
- Apricot Peach Slush 61
- Smooth Strawberry Passion 63
- Wean Off of Soft Drinks 65

CHAPTER 6: MAKE AHEAD SNACKS 66
- Sweet Popcorn Extravaganza 66
- Granola Mini Balls 68
- Homemade Sweet Granola Mix 70
- Healthy Workout Granola Mix 72
- Low-Carb Nachos and Fixings 74
- Crispy Fried Fish with Lemon Sauce 76

CHAPTER 7: LET'S HAVE A PICNIC 78
- Oriental Cabbage Salad 78
- Kickin' Deviled Eggs 80
- Chicken Waldorf Salad 82
- Fresh Green Bean and Tomato Italiano 84
- Confetti Pasta Salad 86
- Cobb Salad with Crab 88

CHAPTER 8: EXCITING DESSERTS 89
- Chocolate Sponge Cake with Strawberries 89
- Luscious Lime Cheesecake Tarts 92
- Fruity Bread Pudding 94
- Almond Ricotta Pudding 96
- Heavenly Chocolate Sorbet 97
- Non Traditional Squash Pie 99

CHAPTER 9: WISE WOK COOKING 101
- Shrimp Egg Rolls 101
- Mandarin Cauliflower and Broccoli Medley 105
- Stir Fry Chicken and Peaches 107
- Oriental Rice 110

Sweet and Sour Shrimp 112
Pears Cardinal 116

CHAPTER 10: LIST OF LOW-CARB FOODS 119

CHAPTER 11: TIPS FOR PREPPING 123

SECTION 2: GRAIN FREE COOKING 130

THE PROBLEM OF GRAINS 132

TRANSITIONING TO A GRAIN FREE DIET 134

A QUESTION OF NUTRITIONAL BALANCE 136

GRAIN FREE SHOPPING AND COOKING TIPS 137

READING THE RECIPE KEY 139

BREAKFAST 140
No-Grain Granola (GF, P, LC) 140
Fresh Homestyle Beef Sausages (GF, P, LC) 142
Almond Cottage Cheese Pancakes (GF, P*, LC**) 144
Open-faced Apple, Egg and Salmon Sandwich (GF, P, LC) 146
Almond Waffles (GF, P*) 147
Green Eggs (GF, P, LC) 149
Hot Porridge (GF, P, LC) 150
No-Grain Breakfast Burritos (GF, P, LC) 151
Sweet Potato Breakfast Casserole (GF, P, LC) 153

MAIN DISHES 155
Pot Roast with Fresh Vegetables (GF, P, LC) 155
Tropical Tilapia (GF, P) 157
Barbecue Chicken with Grain-free Sauce (GF, P) 159
Zucchini Pasta with Roasted Sweet Potatoes and Coconut Pesto (GF, P) ... 161

American Taco Pie (GF, P, LC) 163
Braised Chicken with Sweet Potatoes and Fennel Bulb (GF, P) 165
Baked Cashew Chicken (GF, P, LC) 167
Savory Braised Duck (GF, P, LC) 169
Stuffed Bell Peppers with Veal (GF, P, LC) 171
No-Rice Pad Thai (GF, P, LC) 173

BAKING AND DESSERTS 175

Almond-coconut Chocolate Chip Cookies (GF, P) 175
Honey-Buttermilk Panna Cotta (GF, P*, LC**) 177
No-Grain Sandwich Bread (GF, P, LC) 179
Banana Coconut Muffins (GF, P, LC) 181
No-flour Chocolate Lava Cake (GF, P) 183
Coconut-vanilla Frozen Dessert (GF, P, LC) 185
Almond Flour Blueberry Muffins (GF, P, LC*) 187
Cinnamon Roll Muffins (GF, P) 189
Almond Biscuits (GF, P, LC) 191
Rye-style Flax Bread (GF, P, LC) 193

SNACKS 195

Homemade Yogurt (GF, P, LC*) 195
Roasted Pumpkin Seeds (GF, P, LC) 197
Coconut Chicken Strips (GF, P, LC) 198
Fruit and Nut-Stuffed Pears (GF, P, LC) 200
Sesame Almond Crackers (GF, P, LC) 202
Cheese Crisps (GF, P*, LC) 204
Chicken Cracklings (GF, P, LC) 206

SALADS, SOUPS AND SIDES 207

Creamy Cauliflower Soup (GF, P, LC) 207
Matzoh Ball Soup (GF, P, LC) 208
Split Pea and Mushroom Soup (GF) 210
Squash Oven Fries (GF, P, LC) 212
Cranberry Steak Salad (GF, P, LC) 213
Spinach and Blood Orange Salad (GF, P) 215
Kale Coleslaw (GF, P, LC) 217
Roasted Winter Squash (GF, P, LC) 219

5-DAY GRAIN FREE MEAL PLAN 220

CONCLUSION 223

Introduction

It helps to understand the whys behind the diets and the benefits of each diet starting with the low carb diet plan.

Why Go On a Low Carb Diet

One of the main reasons people go on the low carb diet is to lose weight. Many people find that the low carb diet plan helps them to achieve better results that most any other diet plans. The reason why it works so well is the avoidance and great reduction of the intake of carbohydrates or carbs. When the body ingests carbs, it causes a greater release of insulin into the blood. This causes the cells in the body to absorb the sugar (which is what carbs turn into in the blood stream) and in addition, the body is not prompted to allow the fat to burn because of the presence of excessive carbs. So the body hangs onto the carbs, which builds the fat. It is a vicious cycle causing an epidemic of obesity.

Instead of eating carbs and causing the body to hang onto and build fat, if you have the absence of carbs the body will then look to burning off the fat. A low carb diet sets the body up to be a fat burning machine.

The low carb diet plan does not limit the intake of fat or calories, not like other diet plans such as Weight Watchers. Many people find the calorie and fat limiting plans difficult and often leaves them hungry and rarely satisfied. Because they are hungry, they have less energy to exercise, which is a huge proponent in helping with weight loss. After a couple of days on the low carb diet people find their energy level rises. Their hunger stays satisfied while their body burns the fat and the weight melts away. Protein, which is abundant in the low carb diet plans, help to keep the body satisfied from hunger.

Unlike eating more carbs, when the body ingests more protein, it does not cause a protein addiction. Carbs are very addictive. Protein is not addictive or habit forming, so you can eat it all you want and you will not develop cravings for it as you do for sugary junk food. Proteins help the body to know when it is full so you are less likely to overeat. Carbs causes a frenzy where the body never feels completely full. This is why it is so easy to overeat with carbs. Limiting this very addictive substance will help to stop the over eating and allow the body to get rid of the excessive fat stores.

The Benefits of Grain Free Cooking

The truth is that grains have not been on the human diet chain until the recent 10,000 years. Prior to that our ancestors did not eat grains, nor did they eat legumes. Evidence shows our ancient ancestors were a healthy strong lot of people and probably this stems from their grain free diet. It is true they ate a lot of meat and vegetables and fruits but no grains or beans and peas. Today we eat grains and because of it many suffer from detrimental health issues.

Grain or gluten intolerances and allergies aggravate the digestive system causing symptoms like irritable bowel syndrome, celiac disease, immune issues, and more. Ingesting grains can cause inflammation within the body, which aggravates the cells causing problems. The absence of grains from the diet helps to treat and prevent many of these health concerns.

By avoiding grains, the body will stop the inflammation process (if the grains were causing it in the first place) and many aches and pains and digestive issues will simply go away. Another great benefit to eating a grain free diet is weight loss. Because grains contribute to the amount of carbs we ingest, the absence of grains means the absence of certain carbs. Not only is weight loss attainable it is also easily maintainable.

Meal Planning Success

Just planning meals each week helps to stick with a good diet plan. It is poor planning, or the lack of meal planning, that causes most people to eat the wrong foods. This is why so many suffer from obesity and overweight issues. Being overweight in itself causes the body a lot of harm, from joint and bone issues, to issues with blood pressure, cholesterol, and diabetes and blood sugar problems. By losing the weight, many of these health issues are corrected and prevented from doing further damage to the body.

Successful meal planning starts with a good cookbook like this. You have all the recipes you need to plan a good menu for a couple of weeks in advance if you wish, without repeating recipes. Make a meal plan by listing what you will eat over the next week or two for breakfast, lunch, supper, and even your snacks and desserts. Assess what you already have in your kitchen and pantry and then write the grocery list. Determine about how much the food will cost and get cash for the grocery shopping trip. Leave your checkbook, and credit / debit cards at home. This will help to keep you from straying from the list and impulse buying of junk foods. Stick to your list, purchase your groceries and come home.

It helps to have your recipe book handy and go ahead and prep as much of the food as you can. Chop the vegetables and fruit (that won't go bad), and prepare to cook your meals. Doing this ahead of time makes it easier, especially if you live a busy lifestyle.

Disclaimer

All the advice contained within this book is for informational purposes only. If you have health concerns please seek the advice of your health care provider before taking any advice or starting any new diet plan.

The recipes in this book are adaptations of favorite recipes found all over the web and in popular cookbooks. Many are recipes handed down from word of mouth, family favorites. You may find similar recipes elsewhere but the recipes in this book are unique to this book.

Section 1: Low Carb Diet

Low calorie diet is a general phrase that can have different meanings. Anyone can eat smaller portions of the same foods they are already consuming, but this doesn't adequately justify a low calorie diet. What you eat makes a huge difference in getting the most out of any type of diet. Advertising trends can misrepresent the true meaning of a low calorie diet, while staying within certain truthful perimeters. This book is designed to bring focus on true low calorie diets, that introduce you to a new way of life. Being stronger, healthier and having more energy, is the goal of a successful low calorie diet.

There will be misconceptions addressed, as you read through the chapters. Facts about preservatives, sugar, grains and drinks, will awaken your thoughts about what you are feeding yourself, and your family. The truth is, a low calorie diet is not just for losing weight, but learning how all foods have a direct effect on your body. Just as you know that cigarettes and large amounts of alcohol are harmful, habits of eating certain foods can weaken you immune system, slow down metabolism, and cause fatty tissue to form in your arteries and veins.

You will also find delicious recipes that are just right for stepping into your new life. If you wish to shed a few pounds, mix and match the recipes and portions, according to the carbs. With each recipe made from low-carb foods, and under 500 calories each, the choices are huge.

Why Calorie Counting is a Lie

Keeping calories low should not involve taking out a book and writing down every calorie of food you eat. That gets real boring, real fast. You simply need to know what types of foods can easily be burned off and which ones, cannot. One of the highest forms of calories that is difficult to unload, is sugar. Look at any label and you will see this word.

According to the American Heart Association, no more than 100 calories of sugar should make up a grown woman's diet in one day. This amounts to 6 teaspoons. For a man, 150 calories, or 9 teaspoons, should be the limit. One bowl of whole-grain cereal with milk, contains as much as 9 teaspoons of sugar.

While this may seem downhearted, it gets even worse. Preservatives play a very important role in adding empty calories and high carbs. Take, for example, a box of macaroni and cheese. You may feel that you are being frugal in selecting a product that has cheese, grain, and vitamins, not to mention a shelf life of a year, but here is the ugly truth. Preservatives contain corn syrup, hydrogenated oil, nitrates or sulfates. While consumption of these ingredients can give you a sensation of fullness, they are very difficult for the digestive system to process. Feeling sluggish, developing heart burn and producing fat, are three real symptoms of consuming processed foods. While the package calories may read, 400 calories per serving, is doesn't tell you that these calories are close to impossible to burn off.

You can make it a habit of counting calories, but unless you start with foods that are good for your body, consuming a low carb diet, will be in vein.

Chapter 1: Rise and Shine with a Fortified Breakfast

Crunchy Maple Grape Nuts

Description

Breakfast should contain energy-packed foods to jump start your day. However, in the hustle and bustle of preparing for the day, many people grab a box of cereal. Instead of breaking this habit, keep your own homemade varieties on hand. Low calorie and delicious, these recipes will give your family the right mix of vitamins in a low carb diet. Make ahead and store in airtight containers.

Yields: 12 Servings

Ingredients

3 cups whole wheat flour
1/2 cup barley flour
1/3 cup oat flour
1/3 cup toasted wheat germ
1/2 cup brown sugar

1/2 teaspoon salt
2 teaspoons baking soda
2 teaspoons maple flavoring
1/4 cup heated honey or maple syrup
1/2 cup low-fat milk
2 teaspoons cinnamon

Instructions

1. Warm oven to 325 degrees.

2. Sift and blend dry ingredients

3. In a separate bowl, beat the liquid ingredients together.

4. Stir liquid ingredients into dry ingredients.

5. If the mixture is too watery, work in additional flour.

6, Spread on 2 or 3 baking sheets and bake for 10-15 minutes. After baking, allow to cool, then break up any large clumps and return to oven for an additional 10 minutes.

7. Cool and store in air-tight container.

Healthy Honey Oat Cereal

Description

Here is another version of homemade cereal for those that love to wake up their mouths with lots of crunch and flavor. Nuts, raisins and sweet natural ingredients make this breakfast cereal a great kick start to the day.

Yields: 12 Servings

Ingredients

4 1/2 cups rolled oats
6 Tablespoons sunflower seeds
12 Tablespoons sliced almonds
6 Tablespoons chopped pecans
6 Tablespoons raisins
6 Tablespoons honey
1/4 teaspoon cinnamon
1/4 teaspoon maple extract

Instructions

1. Warm oven to 325 degrees.

2. Place a small pan over a larger pan of boiling water

and add the honey, cinnamon and extract. Heat just until well mixed.

3. Spread baking sheet with aluminum foil and combine all other ingredients (except raisins). You may want to use a baking pan that has a slight lip around the sides, or raise up the edges of the foil to keep dry ingredients from falling off.

4. Using your hands, or a large wooden spoon, mix well, the dry ingredients.

5. Add the honey mixture and coat as much of the dry ingredients as you can.

6. Spread the mixture evenly over the pan and bake for 15 minutes.

7. Remove from oven and let cool. Do not worry if your cereal does not appear crunchy. This comes once it has cooled.

9. After cooling, mix in the raisins and store in an airtight container.

French Toast Strawberry Dippers

Description

Getting kids to the breakfast table is a tough chore. Usually running late, they will grab a finger food, like a doughnut or other gluten-filled treat. Have these quick dippers ready to reach for as they hit the door, and know that they are getting good taste and healthy energy.

Yields: 4 Servings

Ingredients

- 8 slices low-carb sandwich white bread
- 4 Tablespoons softened cream cheese
- 6 fresh, sliced strawberries
- 3 large eggs
- 1/4 cup low-fat milk
- 1 Tablespoon butter
- 1/2 cup maple syrup
- 1/4 cup no-sugar strawberry jam

Instructions

1. Spread cream cheese on 4 slices of bread.

2. Line the cream cheese topping with the sliced strawberries.

3. Top with a bread slice to make a sandwich.

4. In a bowl, mix together the eggs and milk.

5. Use 1/2 of the butter to lightly grease a griddle or skillet and heat on medium.

6. Dip the sandwiches into the egg batter, one at a time, and place in the warmed griddle or skillet.

7. Cook the bread on each side until golden brown. Add remaining butter, if needed.

8. Remove each sandwich, pat with paper towels and cut into 4 long sections.

9. Combine the syrup and jam and heat in a microwave for 30 seconds.

10. Remove and stir well.

11. Place the tasty toast sections in a bread basket, beside the dip, and watch them disappear.

Breakfast Egg Muffins

Description

Use the weekend to cook up a filling and healthy egg breakfast for the day ahead. It will soon become a tradition of a starting a free day, just right, with plenty to go around.

Yields: 8 Servings

Ingredients

8 eggs
½ cup Swiss or Cheddar cheese
½ cup milk
¼ cup chopped onion
¼ cup chopped mushrooms
¼ cup green pepper
¼ cup chopped tomatoes
2 Tablespoons butter
4 plain bagels
8 stale pieces of bread

Instructions

1. Lay out the pieces of bread and cut out the middle in

the shape of a circle. This will serve as a pattern for cooking your egg mixture.

2. In a bowl, whisk the eggs and milk together.

3. Blend in the onion, mushrooms, green pepper and tomatoes.

4. Melt 1 Tablespoon butter in a large skillet and arrange the bread patterns.

5. Pour the egg mixture in the center of each bread pattern, lower heat and cover.

6. After about 4 minutes, remove the cover and sprinkle each round egg with cheese.

7. Add extra butter if needed to keep the bottoms from sticking.

7. Turn off heat and recover skillet.

8. Toast ½ bagel and place on a plate.

9. Carefully remove each egg and peel away the outer bread.

10. Place the round egg on top of the bagel, discarding the bread.

Serve with fresh fruit or a glass of juice.

Cinnamon Raisin Muffins

Description

Nothing can compare to fresh, homemade muffins, right from the oven. These treats will satisfy your craving for bread and sweets, but actually give you less than 150 calories each. Vary the ingredients and have a different selection of muffins each week.

Yields: 12 Servings

Ingredients

1 ½ cups flour
1 ½ teaspoons baking powder
½ teaspoon baking soda
¼ cup butter, refrigerated
1 egg
¼ cup sour cream
¼ cup milk
¼ cup raisins
2 Tablespoons sugar, or sugar substitute
1 teaspoon cinnamon

Instructions

1. Heat oven to 400 degrees F.

2. Combine flour, baking powder and baking soda in large bowl.

3. Cut in the butter until coarse crumbs form.

4. Make a well in the center.

5. In a small bowl, beat the egg, then add the sour cream, milk, raisins, sugar and cinnamon, blending thoroughly.

6. Pour the egg mixture in the center of the flour and mix well.

7. Take a muffin pan and either line with paper muffin holders, or grease lightly.

8. Fill each cup 2/3 full.

9. Bake for 15 minutes, or until browned.

Apple butter or fruit preserves can be used to spread on each muffin.

Asparagus and Mushroom Omelet

Description

This dish makes a meaty and tasty meal for not only breakfast, but lunch, as well. With only 5 grams of carbohydrates and 21 grams of protein, per serving, you will pick up extra energy and not get hungry through the course of the day.

Yields: 4 Servings

Ingredients

8 eggs
8 Tablespoons water
12 stalks fresh asparagus
1 cup sliced mushrooms
1 cup low-fat mozzarella cheese

Instructions

1. In a large skillet, add an inch of water and bring to a boil.

2. Add the asparagus, in two or three different sections, and cook uncovered, just until tender-crisp. Remove and

pat dry.

3. Using a large bowl, whisk the eggs and water.

4. Prepare a large skillet by melting 1 Tablespoon butter.

5. When butter reaches a sizzle over medium-high heat, add ½ of the egg mixture.

6. Cook until the bottom of the egg mixture sets.

7. Carefully lift up the edges with a spatula and allow the uncooked portion to flow out and cook.

8. Once the top is cooked thoroughly, add the asparagus, mushrooms and cheese, and fold into a sandwich with part of the egg.

9. Remove the omelet and cut in half. Repeat with the rest of the egg mixture.

Chapter 2: Lunchtime Recipes for Afternoon Energy

Eggs, Lox and Caramelized Onions on Bagel

Description

Afternoons do not have to be a battle with fatigue and a sluggish feeling. Allow your mid-day meal to recharge your body with fulfilling foods that bring nutrition to your organs and pep up your blood flow. You'll never miss the calories, but you will enjoy missing that afternoon slump that used to slow you down.

Yields: 4 Servings

Ingredients

4 teaspoons butter
1 sliced onion
8 eggs
2 Tablespoons heavy cream
4 ounces lox
4 toasted buns

Instructions

1. Melt 2 teaspoons butter in a skillet, add sliced onions, and cook over medium heat for 8-10 minutes, or until golden brown. Remove to a plate.

2. Beat eggs and cream in a bowl.

3. Melt remaining butter in the skillet and add mixture from bowl.

4. Add salt and pepper, to flavor, and stir constantly, until almost set.

5. Add lox and onions, stirring until heated throughout.

6. Spread on toasted bagel halves.

Silky Onion Soup

Description

Enjoy this tasty soup with a few carrot sticks and a piece of Melba toast. The creamy rich flavor will remind you of an elegant evening meal, instead of a lunch time treat.

Yields: 8 Servings

Ingredients

3 Tablespoons butter
1 sliced onion
2 garlic cloves, minced
2 leeks (white part only), cut in 1/2" strips
1 medium zucchini, sliced
½ teaspoon tarragon
¼ teaspoon salt
¼ teaspoon pepper
2 cups scallions, thinly sliced
28 ounces chicken broth
1 ½ cup water
½ cup heavy cream

Instructions

1. Melt 2 Tablespoons butter in a saucepan, over medium heat.

2. Add onion, garlic, leeks, zucchini, tarragon, salt and pepper.

3. Cover and simmer about 7 minutes
4. Stir in 1 ¾ cup scallions and cook until wilted.

5. Add broth and water and increase the heat until all is boiling.

6. Reduce heat and simmer for 10 minutes.

7. Remove from heat and break up the vegetables with a masher.

8. Return to a medium heat and add the remaining butter and the cream.

9. Heat just until boiling begins.

10. Remove from heat and sprinkle with remaining scallions.

Makes a great make ahead meal for warming up when on the run.

Tuna Salad Supreme in Tortilla Shells

Description

Give new meaning to tired tuna salad that grows old after a time or two. The right mix of veggies and a complementary bowl will turn tuna into a sought after lunch.

Yields: 4 Servings

Ingredients

4 8-inch round flour tortillas
1 Tablespoon olive oil
3 5-ounce cans Albacore tuna, drained
6 stalks celery, chopped
1 cucumber, peeled and cubed
2/3 cup mayonnaise
16 cherry tomatoes, quartered
4 lettuce leaves

Instructions

1. Heat oven to 400-degrees.

2. Take 4 oven-proof bowls and turn upside down.

3. Brush both sides of the tortillas with olive oil and place one over each bowl.

4. Bake in the oven until the tortillas are crisp and hold their shape, about 7 to 10 minutes.

5. Remove from oven and keep draped over the bowls until completely cooled.

6. In a bowl, mix the remaining ingredients (except the lettuce leaves).

7. Invert the bowls and lace each one with a lettuce leaf before adding the tuna salad.

You will never eat tuna salad on bread again!

Low-Cal Greek Salad

Description

Never miss out on the taste of feta cheese, blended perfectly in a luscious bed of romaine lettuce. Here is a great way to give in to your taste bud desires, without adding unwanted carbohydrates.

Yields: 1 Serving

Ingredients

8 leaves romaine lettuce, torn
1 cucumber, peeled and sliced
1 chopped tomato
½ cup red onion, sliced
½ cup low-fat feta cheese, crumbled
2 Tablespoons olive oil
2 Tablespoons fresh lemon juice
1 teaspoon dried oregano leaves
½ teaspoon salt

Instructions

1. Mix torn lettuce, cucumber, tomato, onion, and cheese in a large serving bowl.

2. Using a separate bowl, whisk together the oil, lemon juice, oregano, and salt.

3. Pour over salad.

Spinach Salad with Chicken and Raspberry

Description

Raspberry adds a tangy flavor to salads and chicken, so why not combine them? Adding a few other tricks will make this mid-day meal something to look forward to.

Yields: 4 Servings

Ingredients

¼ cup white vinegar
5 Tablespoons olive oil
1 teaspoon honey
½ teaspoon orange peel, shredded
½ teaspoon salt
¼ teaspoon pepper
4 skinless, boneless chicken breast halves
5 cups torn spinach
5 cups torn mixed greens
1 cup fresh raspberries
1 papaya, peeled, seeded and cubed

Instructions

1. Combine the vinegar, 4 Tablespoons olive oil, honey,

orange peel, salt and pepper.

2. Pour into an airtight jar and shake well. Store in the refrigerator to chill.

3. In a large skillet, heat over medium heat and add the remaining oil .

4. Add the chicken breasts and cook for 10 to 15 minutes, turning often, to brown all sides.

5. When no longer pink, remove from the skillet and pat out any excess oil and water.

6. Cut the warm chicken into thin strips.

7. In a large bowl, toss the greens, spinach and chicken strips.

8. Take your salad dressing and pour over the salad, tossing well.

9. Add the raspberries and cubed papaya, tossing gently.

Lettuce Roll-Ups with Pumpkin Seed Pate

Description

Move over hamburgers. This flavorful rendition of what used to be a sandwich, will make you wonder why anyone would choose meat over fresh veggies. Filled with marinated vegetables and seasoned with a unique pate, all your friends will want your recipe.

Yields: 6 Servings

Ingredients

6 large lettuce leaves

Marinated Vegetables:

2 stalks celery, sliced in 2-inch strips
1 cup carrots, shredded
¼ cup red onion, thinly sliced
2 Tablespoons flax oil
2 teaspoons lemon juice

Pate:

1 ½ garlic cloves

juice from 1 squeezed lemon
1 cup pumpkin seeds, soaked and sprouted
¼ cup flax oil
¾ teaspoon salt
¼ cup fresh parsley
¼ cup fresh basil
¼ cup dill
1/8 teaspoon turmeric
½ teaspoon fresh rosemary

Instructions for Pate

1. Using a food processor, place the garlic and pumpkins seeds inside and chop.

2. Add the lemon juice and mix until creamy.

3. Add the herbs and seasonings.

4. Pulse to finely chop all the herbs.

5. Spoon into a bowl.

Instructions for Assembly

1. Place all ingredients for marinated vegetables in a medium bowl and coat all pieces.

2. Lay flat a lettuce leaf and spread on a generous amount of pate.

3. Add ½ cup of marinated vegetables.

4. Roll up, folding the top and bottom to secure.

Chapter 3: Great Dinner Surprises

Mushroom Laced Meatballs

Description

You don't have to tell the family that they are on a low calorie diet when serving up dishes that are guaranteed to hit the spot. Lean hamburger will be anything, but boring, when dressed up with the right spices. See if anyone believes you when you admit that this dish has only 300 calories per serving.

Yields: 6 Servings

Ingredients

1 pound ground beef
1 egg
1/2 cup whole wheat bread crumbs
4 ounces shredded cheddar cheese
1/4 cup onion, chopped
1 Tablespoon Worcestershire sauce
1 Tablespoon fresh parsley, chopped

1/2 teaspoon basil
1/2 teaspoon pepper
1 Tablespoon oil
1 cup sliced mushrooms
1/2 cup beef broth
1/2 cup cooking wine

Instructions

1. Mix together meat, egg, bread crumbs, cheese, onion, Worcestershire sauce, parsley, basil and pepper.

2. Shape into 12 meatballs.

3. Add oil to skillet and brown meatballs on all sides, about 5 minutes.

4. Remove meatballs and dry on paper towels.

5. Add mushrooms to the drippings in the skillet and cook over medium heat for 2 to 3 minutes.

6. In a small bowl, mix flour, broth and wine until blended.

7. Pour over mushrooms and cook until boiling, stirring constantly.

8. Turn down heat and simmer sauce for 2 minutes.

9. Add meatballs to the creamy mixture and warm thoroughly, before serving.

Sassy Cheese and Chicken Enchiladas

Description

Kids will come running when they smell the succulent aroma of one of their favorite meals. Chicken enchiladas always top the favorites list, especially when dripping with cheese sauce. Microwave the entire meal and save time.

Yields: 6 Servings

Ingredients

2 cups cooked chicken breasts, chopped
1/2 cup chopped onion
1 garlic clove, minced
1 Tablespoon oil
4 ounces chopped green chilies
1/2 cup chicken broth
2 teaspoons chili powder
1 teaspoon cumin
4 ounces cubed cream cheese
6 6-inch flour tortillas
1/4 pound Colby or Cheddar cheese, cubed
2 Tablespoons milk
1/2 cup fresh chopped tomato

Instructions

1. In a 2-quart microwavable dish, mix onion, garlic and oil.

2. Microwave on high for 2 minutes. Stir and return for 1 more minute.

3. Remove and add chicken, chilies, broth and seasonings. Blend well.

4. Return to microwave and cook on high for 4 minutes.

5. Remove and add cream cheese, stirring until all the cheese is melted.

6. Spoon 1/2 cup of the mixture onto a tortilla shell and roll up. Repeat 6 times and place all, seam side down, on a flat microwavable dish.

7. In a clean microwavable dish, mix the Colby or Cheddar cheese, milk and 1/4 cup tomato and microwave on high for 1 minute. Stir and return for another 1 or 2 minutes.

8. Remove the cheese sauce and pour over the

enchiladas.

9. Microwave on high for 4 minutes.

10. Remove and top with remaining tomatoes.

11. Return to the microwave and cook on high for another 2 to 3 minutes.

Serve with salsa and chips.

Colorful Veggie Meatloaf

Description

Put sparkle in an old dish by using creative, and healthy vegetables. This one dish meal will add new meaning to meatloaf, as it was once known.

Yields: 8 Servings

Ingredients

1 1/2 pounds lean ground beef
3 cups white bread crumbs, toasted
1 cup diced tomatoes
1 cup fresh or frozen green beans (thawed)
1 egg
1 carrot
2 Tablespoons Worcestershire sauce
1 1/2 teaspoons salt
1/4 teaspoon pepper
1/4 cup ketchup

Instructions

1. Preheat oven to 375 degrees F
2. In a large bowl, mix all ingredients (except ketchup),

until well blended.

3. Turn into a loaf pan and top with ketchup.

4. Bake for 50 to 60 minutes, or until cooked throughout.

5. Remove and transfer to a platter, patting dry any excess fat.

Serve with a tossed salad for a filling, low calorie dinner.

Grilled Summer Kabobs

Description

Grilling during the spring and summer months can be exciting. The smell of meat that is char-broiled to perfection, can get your tummy growling. Make a delightful and low carb dinner, while including steak. A little bit goes a long way with this recipe.

Yields: 6 Servings

Ingredients

1 1/2 pounds boneless beef sirloin steak, cut into strips
1 zucchini, cut in 1-inch pieces
1 squash, cut into diagonal pieces
2 onions, quartered
12 cherry tomatoes
1/2 cup mayonnaise
1/2 cup plain yogurt
1/4 cup lemon juice
3 cloves garlic, minced
2 teaspoons minced ginger root
1/2 teaspoon cardamom
1/2 teaspoon cumin
1/2 teaspoon coriander

1/8 teaspoon red pepper

Instructions

1. Prepare the marinade by blending all seasonings, mayonnaise, yogurt and lemon juice. Put 1/2 cup of dressing aside for later.

2. Skewer the steak strips between the zucchini, squash, onions, and tomatoes.

3. Place the kabobs on a hot grill and brush with the marinade.

4. Grill for 10 or 15 minutes, or until the meat reaches the required doneness, turning and brushing twice.

5. Remove and serve with the reserved dressing.

Veggie Laced Macaroni and Cheese

Description

Macaroni and Cheese, from a box, offers little in the way of low carbs and vitamins. However, it will not take long for family to miss this simple mix of cheese and pasta. Try this homemade version that has a new twist and watch them ask for more.

Yields: 4 Servings

Ingredients

9 ounces penne noodles
1 ½ cups sharp cheddar cheese
1 Tablespoon tarragon
1/8 teaspoon ground white pepper
4 carrots, peeled and sliced
juice from one fresh orange
¼ cup water

Instructions

Warm oven to 350 degrees F.

In a saucepan, combine the carrots and juice from

orange.

Add 1/4 cup water and heat until boiling.

Turn down, cover and simmer for about 30 minutes.

Remove from heat and transfer to a blender.

Puree contents.

In a separate pan, boil the penne noodles in salted water until al dente.

Drain off the water, reserving 1 cup in the pan.

Add the drained pasta to the pan, along with the puree.

Heat on medium, stirring to coat penne.

Cook, stirring often,
Add 1 cup cheese, tarragon and white pepper.

Once the mixture becomes creamy, pour all into a greased baking dish.

Add the remaining cheese on top and bake for 20 minutes.

Remove and let stand for 5 minutes before serving.

Chapter 4: Unique Side Dishes

Fake Mashed Potatoes

Description

If your family craves meat and potatoes, this is just an old habit. However, you can give them what they want by serving a meat dish and using this unique recipe for mashed potatoes, made from fresh cauliflower. The flavor will be better, the consistency, fluffy, and that mindset of meat and potatoes will quickly dissipate.

Yields: 4 Servings

Ingredients

1 fresh cauliflower head
1 Tablespoon water
1 Tablespoon butter
2 Tablespoons heavy cream

Instructions

Chop cauliflower into small pieces and add to a large casserole dish.

Add 1 Tablespoon water, cover, and microwave on high for 5 minutes.

Remove and let stand for 5 minute.

Drain water from cauliflower and place in a food processor.

Add butter and heavy cream.

Process until smooth.

Scoop out and place in a serving bowl.

Simplistic Green Beans

Description

Sometimes the best things in life are amazingly simple. Take this green bean dish, for example. Only two ingredients deliver taste and fulfillment, complimenting any main dish.

Yields: 4 Servings

Ingredients

1 pound fresh green beans
1 onion, cut in half and sliced thick
1 Tablespoon oil
2 Tablespoons butter
Unrefined sea salt and pepper to taste

Instructions

Using a heavy skillet, sauté green beans, over medium heat, in oil and 1 Tablespoon of butter.

Add onion pieces and continue sautéing until the onions brown.

Turn into a serving bowl and let guests season, to their liking, with salt and pepper.

Dressy Cauliflower Casserole

Description

Cauliflower is a great food for keeping carbs low, but can become quite boring when prepared over and over again. This recipe dresses up this vegetable by using other seasonings for a flavor that almost makes you forget about the main ingredient.

Yields: 6 Servings

Ingredients

1 fresh head cauliflower, broken up, or 1 16 ounce frozen bag, cooked and drained
½ cup onion, diced
1 ½ cup fresh mushrooms
2 Tablespoons butter
¼ cup heavy cream
¼ cup mayonnaise
4 ounces shredded cheddar cheese
¼ cup green onions, chopped

Instructions

Warm oven to 350 degrees F.

Place prepared cauliflower in a greased 2-quart casserole dish.

In a skillet, sauté onion and mushrooms in the butter.

Add to the cauliflower and mix.

Mix in cheese.

In a small bowl, combine cream and mayonnaise.

Pour the sauce over the cauliflower mix and coat well.

Sprinkle the top with green onions.

Bake, covered, for 25 minutes.

Remove lid and bake another 10 minutes, or until the top is brown and crispy.

Chapter 5: Fulfillment with Drinks

Pina Colada Smoothie

Description

Soft drinks and some fruit drinks can be loaded with sugar. By side-stepping this calorie boosting substance, drinks take on a more lasting flavor, keep you from tiring and give your body the liquids that they need.

Yields: 2 Servings

Ingredients

1/2 cup unsweetened coconut milk
1/4 cup plain yogurt
1/2 cup fresh pineapple chunks
1/4 teaspoon coconut extract
1 teaspoon fresh lime juice
8 ice cubes
2 packets sugar substitute

2 lime slices

Instructions

1. In a blender, add all ingredients (except lime slices).

2. Blend on high until smooth.

Add a slice of lime to the edge of each glass to add a zesty twist.

Refreshing Fruit Shake

Description

Shakes do not have to weigh you down with unhealthy calories and leaving you feel sluggish. Try this homemade version of a strawberry milkshake and forget the tired feeling. Double the recipe to share with a friend.

Yields: 1 Serving

Ingredients

1 cup strawberries
1 cup almond flavored low-fat milk
1 packet sugar substitute
1 cube tofu
1 cup ice cubes

Instructions

1. Blend together strawberries, milk, sugar substitute, and tofu in a blender.

2. Add ice cubes and blend again.

Awesome Juice Spritzer

Description

Keeping the kids (and adults) away from soft drinks can be a never ending chore. Keep a 2-liter bottle of refreshing juice spritzer in the frig and no one will even miss the pop.

Yields: 6 Servings

Ingredients

9 ounces pineapple, orange, or pomegranate juice
48 ounces club soda or sparkling water

Instructions

1. Add juice to club soda or sparkling water, using a 2 liter air tight bottle.

Freshly processed and strained fruit can also be used in the place of juice.

Honey Dew Smoothie

Description

Add variety to your beverages by using a little thought of ingredient. The flavor will bring a new twist to boring fruit juices. Light and healthy, this drink only has 110 calories per serving. Increase ingredients to share with family and friends.

Yields: 2 Servings

Ingredients

4 cups cubed honey dew
2 apples, peeled, cored and cubed
2 kiwi fruits, peeled and sliced
3 packets sugar substitute
2 Tablespoons lemon juice
2 cups ice cubes

Instructions

1. Combine all ingredients (except ice cubes) in a blender and blend well.

2. Add ice cubes and blend until ice becomes broken

into small pieces.

Apricot Peach Slush

Description

This fruity drink has become a favorite of diabetics because of the sweet flavor and smooth texture. It's hard to think that something so refreshing can be good for you, but it is. Keep plenty of apricot nectar on hand because this beverage will go fast.

Yields: 6 Servings

Ingredients

15 ½ ounces apricot nectar, chilled
2 fresh peaches, peeled, pitted and sliced
1 ½ cups crushed ice
1 Tablespoon lemon juice
1 ½ cups chilled carbonated water

Instructions

1. In a blender, combine the apricot nectar, peaches, lemon juice and crushed ice.

2. Blend until smooth.

3. Spoon into a tall glass, filling halfway.

4. Fill the glass to the top with carbonated water.

Smooth Strawberry Passion

Description

Forget the milkshakes and all the calories and instead, make up a batch of Smooth Strawberry Passion drinks. Low in carbs and fat, this drink is great for a gathering or just to sit on the porch on a hot summer day.

Yields: 6 Servings

Ingredients

4 cups fresh strawberries, sliced
1 banana
1 kiwi fruit
16 ounces vanilla yogurt
1 cup ice cubes

Instructions

Using a blender, add strawberries, banana, and yogurt.

Blend until creamy.

Add ice cubes, one at a time, blending until they are broken up.

Pour in glasses, garnishing with kiwi fruit.

Wean Off of Soft Drinks

In a world of perfection, you would cut out all soda. The sugary sweeteners, found in soda, is almost impossible to break down. However, the addiction to soft drinks can cause you to abandon a new eating plan, after a day or two. If you currently have sugary soda in your daily life, definitely change to a diet brand - but don't try to cut it out cold turkey. You want to succeed in your new diet, so it is okay to start out slow. Slowly wean yourself off of the addictive, artificial taste by trading for a more refreshing taste of natural ingredients.

Chapter 6: Make Ahead Snacks

Sweet Popcorn Extravaganza

Description

Showtime in front of the TV will become even more exciting when there is a big bowl of crunchy, sweet snacks ready for each turn. Make this light and wholesome finger food ahead of time and keep in an air tight container.

Yields: 8 Servings

Ingredients

4 Tablespoons butter, melted
2 egg whites
2 packets sugar substitute
½ teaspoon vanilla extract
½ teaspoon cinnamon
¼ teaspoon salt
1 ½ cups low-carb cereal flakes
3 ounces pecans or almonds
4 cups pop corn

Instructions

1. Heat oven to 300 degrees F.

2. Lay a sheet of aluminum foil over a baking sheet and spray with Canola oil.

3. In a small bowl, combine butter, egg whites, sugar substitute, vanilla, cinnamon and salt.

4. Whisk the egg mixture until well blended.

5. Using a large bowl, add cereal and nuts and coat with the melted butter.

6. Add popcorn and lightly toss.

7. Pour mixture onto the baking sheet and spread evenly.

8. Bake for 20 to 25 minutes, or until crispy.

9. Remove and cool.

Store in an air tight container until show time. By adding the popcorn to the mixture last, there will be less clumps for hands to grab.

Granola Mini Balls

Description

These little bundles are the perfect size for snacking or grabbing as a quick energy picker-upper. Leave a plateful on the table and the refrigerator door will have less activity.

Yields: 6 Servings

Ingredients

2 cups granola
½ cup raisins
½ cup pecans, chopped
½ cup dried apricots
1 cup low-fat dried milk
1 cup creamy peanut butter
1/3 cup honey

Instructions

1. In a large bowl, mix granola, raisins, pecans, apricots, dried milk, and honey.

2. Gradually add peanut butter, stirring until all

ingredients are well covered.

3. Using your hands, form into small balls and place on small squares of waxed paper.

4. Place the balls, including the waxed paper on a serving plate. The waxed paper will keep the balls from sticking to one another.

Homemade Sweet Granola Mix

Description

Teach your kids how to have a great snack by letting them help make this sweet, crunchy treat. They will learn how to eat healthier, plus have something to munch on while playing video games.

Yields: 8 Servings

Ingredients

1 cup rolled oats
1 cup almonds
1 cup unsalted peanuts
1 cup raw sunflower seeds
1 cup flax seeds
1 cup sweetened coconut flakes
1 cup dried cranberries
3 Tablespoons brown sugar syrup

Instructions

1. Preheat oven to 250 degrees F.

2. Line a baking sheet with parchment sheets.

3. Use a large mixing bowl and add all ingredients.

4. Mix well with a wooden spoon or spatula.

5. Spread onto the baking sheet and flatten.

6. Bake for 15 minutes.

7. Remove and break up the granola pieces.

8. Bake for an additional 15 minutes.

9. Remove and cool.

10. Place into an airtight container.

Healthy Workout Granola Mix

Description

Here is another type of granola treat that is favored by athletes after a good workout. However, it was soon found to be a favorite of youngsters, as well.

Yields: 8 servings

Ingredients

1 cup rolled oats
1 cup almonds
1 cup dried cranberries
1 ½ cups butter
½ cup brown sugar
2 Tablespoons honey
½ teaspoon vanilla extract

Instructions

1. Preheat oven to 375 degrees F.

2. Coat baking tray with spray canola oil
3. In a large bowl, combine the oats, almonds, dried cranberries, and ground cinnamon.

4. Blend well with a large wooden spoon or spatula.

5. Add the butter, brown sugar, honey and vanilla extract together in a separate bowl, blending well.

6. Pour the butter mixture into the dry ingredients and mix until all is coated.

7. Spread the mixture onto the greased baking tray and press down to flatten.

8. Place in the oven for 20 to 25 minutes.

9. Remove and cool.

10. Either cut into bars, or break up the pieces for a bite size treat.

Low-Carb Nachos and Fixings

Description

Many people admit that their toughest part of staying on a low-carb diet, is giving up chips. Here is a unique way to have it all. Chips, cheese, salsa, at an amazing 6.5 net carbs. The secret is in the chips and here is a way to have your cake and eat it, too.

Yields: 10 Servings

Ingredients

8 ounces low-carb soy chips
1 cup chopped black olives
4 ½ ounces chopped, mild green chilies
12 ounces cheddar cheese, grated
2/3 cup sour cream
2/3 cup salsa

Instructions

1. Move rack in oven to within 6 inches of the broiler and preheat to broil.

2. Line 2 baking sheets with aluminum foil and spray

lightly, with canola oil spray.

3. Arrange the soy chips on the baking sheets in a single layer.

4. Top each chip with olives and chilies.

5. Sprinkle with cheese.

6. Place in oven and broil for 45 to 60 seconds.

7. Remove and transfer to a platter.

8. Place sour cream in one small bowl and the salsa in another.

9. Serve together.

Crispy Fried Fish with Lemon Sauce

Description

Who says you can't have fried fish on a low-carb diet? Choose pollock, whiting, haddock or scrod, and don't forget the sauce.

Yields: 4 Servings

Ingredients

4 8-ounce fish fillets
1 egg
2 ounces baked potato chips, ground
2 Tablespoons water
2 Tablespoons canola oil
½ cup mayonnaise
3 Tablespoons fresh dill, chopped
2 teaspoons lemon zest, grated
¼ teaspoon pepper

Instructions

1. Spread chip crumbs on a flat surface lined with waxed paper.

2. In a wide bowl, whisk 1 egg with water and brush on each fillet.

3. Heat a non-stick skillet to medium heat and add 1 Tablespoon canola oil

4. Dredge each fillet through the crumbs and place in the hot skillet.

5. Turn each fillet once after cooking about 3 to 4 minutes, or until golden brown.

6. Gently remove to plates
7. In a small bowl, mix the mayonnaise, dill, zest and pepper for dip.

Chapter 7: Let's Have a Picnic

Oriental Cabbage Salad

Description

Summer comes with lots of potlucks and bar-b-ques. Trying to watch your eating habits can be very trying with hamburgers and hot dogs being served. Start bringing great side dishes to get togethers and introduce the crowd to great tasting foods.

Yields: 4 Servings

Ingredients

½ head grated, green cabbage
3 chopped scallions
2 Tablespoons sesame oil
2 Tablespoons rice wine vinegar
2 Tablespoons toasted sesame seeds

Instructions

1. In a large serving bowl, combine the cabbage, scallions, oil and vinegar.

2. Toss well, then refrigerate.

3. Right before serving, add the sesame seeds and toss lightly.

Kickin' Deviled Eggs

Description

Deviled eggs are an all-time favorite at picnics, but these beauties will make the crowd stop and say, WOW! The special ingredient may surprise you, and certainly, anyone who indulges. With 1 gram of carbs and 178 calories, maybe it won't hurt to have a couple.

Yields: 20 eggs

Ingredients

10 large eggs
4 Tablespoons cream cheese
½ cup mayonnaise
2 Tablespoons fresh chives, minced
2 teaspoons wasabi paste
pepper
1 teaspoon sea salt

Instructions

1. Boil eggs in a single layer, using a large saucepan, for 7 minutes.

2. Turn off heat and cover saucepan for 15 minutes.

3. Drain water off and refill with cold water. Let stand for at least 10 minutes.

4. Peel eggs and cut in half, long way.

5. Remove yolks and place in a large bowl.

6. Add the cream cheese and wasabi paste.

7. Mash with a fork or masher until everything is blended and resembles small crumbs.

8. Stir in the mayonnaise and chives and add pepper to taste.

9. Place the yolk mixture in a pastry bag and squeeze filling into the white cups of the eggs.

10. Make a swirling motion, beginning with the outer layer and working to a point in the middle.

11. Just before serving, sprinkle with sea salt.

Chicken Waldorf Salad

Description

Everyone loves the flavor of apples and walnuts, mixed with greens and a tart dressing. Make it a meal by adding chicken and using a new kind of dressing that will make guests request, time and time again.

Yields: 4 Servings

Ingredients

4 cooked and cubed chicken breasts
1 cup chopped celery
1 ½ cup chopped apples
4 ounces walnut pieces
4 Tablespoons raisins
1 cup low-fat Italian dressing
10 cups Iceberg and Bibb lettuce

Instructions

1. Place the lettuce, chicken, apples and celery in a large serving bowl and toss well.

2. Pour the Italian dressing over all and toss to coat.

3. Add the walnut pieces and raisins, gently blending.

Fresh Green Bean and Tomato Italiano

Description

There is nothing more flavorful than the taste of fresh green beans that are served up steamed and crunchy. Bring this dish to your outdoor party and you will find that even the youngsters will be tempted with their presence. This is a quick and easy side dish that delivers a compliment to any type of meat.

Yields: 6 Servings

Ingredients

3 cups fresh green beans
2 plum tomatoes, sliced into thin wedges
2 Tablespoons fresh basil
¼ cup Italian dressing

Instructions

1. Steam green beans for 10 minutes, just long enough to remove the raw texture.

2. Cool and add tomatoes and basil.

3. Pour dressing over all and toss lightly, just to coat.

Confetti Pasta Salad

Description

Here is a dish that is almost too beautiful to eat. Colorful and robust, it will seem more like a main dish than a complimentary side. Increase the size to share for an outdoor BBQ or other picnic event.

Yields: 4 Servings

Ingredients

1 cup multicolored, low-carb penne, cooked
4 artichoke hearts, diced
4 ounces thinly sliced turkey breast strips
8 ounces fresh mozzarella, diced
4 Tablespoon red pepper
8 Tablespoons fresh, chopped green beans
4 Tablespoons olive oil
4 teaspoons balsamic vinegar
2 teaspoons fresh oregano, chopped

Instructions

1. Combine pasta, artichoke hearts, turkey, mozzarella, red pepper and green beans in a large salad bowl.

2. In a small bowl, mix oil, vinegar, and oregano.

3. Pour over the pasta mixture and toss.

Cobb Salad with Crab

Description

Seafood is the main ingredient that gives this salad a wonderful flavor. Along with other cobb salad favorite additions, this side dish goes very well with those lake-caught fish.

Yields: 4 Servings

Ingredients

12 cups romaine lettuce, torn into bite-size pieces
12 ounce cooked crab meat
2 cups cherry tomatoes, halved
1 cup crumbled blue cheese
½ cup olive oil raspberry flavored dressing

Instructions

1. In a large serving bowl, add lettuce, crab meat, tomatoes and blue cheese.

2. Toss well then add dressing and toss again.

Chapter 8: Exciting Desserts

Chocolate Sponge Cake with Strawberries

Description

There is something wrong with a low-carb diet that does not allow for the sweet pleasures in life, mainly cake and chocolate. This dessert will satisfy both with rich flavor and texture.

Yields: 10 Servings

Ingredients

7 egg whites
1/8 tsp cream of tartar
¾ cup sugar
3 egg yolks
1 teaspoon vanilla
1 cup cake flour
3 Tablespoons melted butter
1 ½ ounces semisweet chocolate
2 Tablespoons canola oil
12 plump strawberries

Instructions

1. Heat oven to 350 degr F.

2. Use a large bowl to beat the egg whites and cream of tartar until foamy.

3. Add the sugar, gradually, while whipping into a meringue, with soft peaks.

4. In another bowl, beat together the egg yolks and vanilla.

5. Add the egg yolk mixture to the egg whites, gradually, folding until well blended.

6. Fold in the flour, stirring until all has been absorbed.

7. Pour batter into the cake batter and fold gently.

9. Spoon the batter into a 10-inch tube pan and bake for 35-40 minutes, or until the center proves clean, with a tooth pick.

10. Remove the cake and turn upside down on a large bottle so all sides are exposed to the air.

11. Cool for about an hour.

12. Remove the pan and run a knife along the sides of the pan to loosen the cake, then invert onto a wire rack to further cool.

13. Place on a serving dish.

14. Melt the chocolate and oil, slowly to keep from scorching and drizzle over the cooled cake.

15. Dot the top with strawberries.

Luscious Lime Cheesecake Tarts

Description

Cheesecake can add the final touch to a great meal, or be a special treat for friends that visit. Adding the tartness of lime and the sweetness of kiwi, will let you savor every bite.

Yields: 12 Servings

Ingredients

12 vanilla wafers
¾ cup cottage cheese
8 ounces low-fat cream cheese
¼ cup sugar or sugar substitute
2 eggs
1 Tablespoon grated lime rind
1 Tablespoon fresh lime juice
1 teaspoon vanilla
¼ cup vanilla flavored yogurt
2 kiwis, peeled, sliced and halved

Instructions

1. Using a 12-cup muffin pan, line each cup with a paper

muffin liner.

2. Heat oven to 350 degrees F.

3. Place a vanilla wafer in the bottom of each cup.

4. Using a blender, add the cottage cheese, cream cheese and sugar. Blend well.

5. Add the eggs, lime rind, lime juice and vanilla. Beat until smooth.

6. Spoon the mixture into the lined muffin cups and bake for 15-20 minutes, or until well set.

7. Remove from oven and chill completely.

8. Right before serving, spread the vanilla flavored yogurt on top and garnish with kiwi pieces.

Fruity Bread Pudding

Description

Bread pudding can become a sinful dish when laced with peaches and cream. Serve up this delightful dessert to family and friends. Have the recipe ready to share because everyone will want to know your secret ingredients.

Yields: 12 Servings

Ingredients

1 teaspoon butter, softened
6 slices low-carb bread, cubed
1 ½ cups fresh or frozen chopped peaches
4 eggs
1 cup heavy cream
½ cup sugar
¼ teaspoon nutmeg
1 ½ teaspoons vanilla
2 Tablespoons sliced almonds

Instructions

1. Warm oven to 350 F degrees.

2. Butter an 8-inch square baking dish

3. Add bread crumbs and peaches to dish and toss.

4. In a medium-sized bowl, add eggs, cream, sugar, nutmeg and vanilla, and whisk together.

5. Pour the egg mixture over the bread and peaches.

6. Let stand for 10 minutes to allow the bread to absorb the liquid mixture.

7. Sprinkle almonds on top of the dish.

8. Place the dish inside a 9x11 pan, filled with boiling water. The water should rise halfway up the sides of the 8-inch dish.

9. Bake for 45 to 50 minutes, or until a clean knife shows that it is done.

Almond Ricotta Pudding

Description

Take a break with a smooth, luscious pudding that is satisfying and only 8 carbs per serving. Quick to make, this recipe is designed for 1 serving but can be stretched to include the whole family.

Yields: 1 Serving

Ingredients

½ cup ricotta cheese
¼ teaspoon almond extract
1 packet sweetener
1 teaspoon slivered toasted almonds

Instructions

1. Mix the ricotta cheese, almond extract and sugar substitute.

2. Sprinkle with almonds.

Enjoy.

Heavenly Chocolate Sorbet

Description

Remember the fudge ice pops that you enjoyed as a child? Here is an adult version that will bring back memories, yet satisfy the grown up you. You will need an ice-cream maker for this recipe. This treat is not for kids, the more reason to sneak away and enjoy.

Yields: 4 Servings

Ingredients

2 cups ice cold water
1 teaspoon unflavored gelatin
1 ½ cups sugar-free chocolate syrup
1 cup low-fat milk
3 Tablespoons dark rum

Instructions

1. Add 2 Tablespoons ice water in a glass measuring cup.

2. Sprinkle with gelatin.

3. Microwave for 20 seconds to dissolve the gelatin.

3. In a medium-sized bowl, add ¾ cup syrup, the remaining ice water, milk and rum.

4. Stir until blended.

5. Add the remaining chocolate syrup into the mix and whisk.

6. Add the dissolved gelatin and stir.

7. Pour the mixture into an ice-cream maker and churn, according to instructions.

8. Remove and place in an airtight container and place in the freezer until ready to serve.

Non Traditional Squash Pie

Description

Pumpkin pie may be the tradition, but there's a new version in town. Serve up this wonderful dessert that offers much lower calories and carbs and start a new traditional during the holidays, or any time.

Yields: 8 Servings

Ingredients

3 cups cooked winter squash, mashed
¾ cup unsweetened coconut milk
¼ cup honey
3 eggs
2 teaspoons pumpkin pie spice
1 ½ teaspoons maple extract
1 ½ Tablespoons arrowroot powder
1 ¼ teaspoons unrefined sea salt, finely ground
½ teaspoon sugar

Instructions

1. Warm oven to 350 degr F.

2. Mix all ingredients with a mixer or in a food processor. If the consistency is too thick, add a little water, 1 teaspoon each, until no longer stiff.

3. Pour into a greased 10-inch pie pan and bake for 50 to 60 minutes, or until a knife comes out clean, when placed in the center.

4. Allow pie to cool then chill for another 30 minutes, to firm.

Chapter 9: Wise Wok Cooking

Shrimp Egg Rolls

Description

Reintroduce your wok to keep fat and sugar limited. It may take some time to prepare these awesome egg rolls, but the results are well worth the trouble.

Yields: 8 Servings

Ingredients

½ pounds raw shrimp, cleaned and deveined
1 teaspoon sherry
1 teaspoon salt
½ teaspoon cornstarch
3 Tablespoons canola oil
3 cups diced celery
½ teaspoon sugar
1 Tablespoon water
½ cup fresh bean sprouts
1 cup shredded lettuce
1 cup chopped water chestnuts
16 egg-roll wrappers

Instructions

1. In a small bowl, combine shrimp, sherry, salt and cornstarch.

2. Let the mixture marinate for 12 to minutes.

3. Heat 1 tablespoon oil in work.

4. Add shrimp mixture and stir-fry until shrimp is pink and firm.

5. Remove to a mixing bowl.

6. Add remaining oil to wok and add celery, stir-frying for 2 to 3 minutes.

7. Add sugar and water.

8. Cover and let steam for 1 minute.

9. Remove cover and stir-fry until all the liquid has evaporated.

10. Add to shrimp mixture.

11. Add remaining ingredients.

12. Blend well.

13. Prepare wrappers by laying out flat.

14. Fill each one with ¼ cup shrimp mixture.

15. Lift lower triangle of wrapper over filling and tuck the point under.

16. Leave the upper point of the wrapper flat.

17. Bring the 2 end flaps up and over the enclosed filling and press flaps down firmly.

18. Brush cold water over the exposed triangles and roll the filled portion until you have a neat package. The water will seal your ingredients protectively.

19. Repeat until you have 16 filled egg rolls.

20. Fill the wok with 3 inches of oil in the center.

21. Heat to 375 degrees F.

22. Using tongs, lower 4 eggs rolls into the oil and deep

fry for 3 to 4 minutes, or until golden brown.

23. Drain on paper towels, blotting out all of the oil.

24. Repeat until all egg rolls have been cooked.

Serve with hot mustard, plum sauce or soy sauce. You can also store for later use by cooling and wrapping in plastic wrap, then placing in freezer bags to refrigerate or freeze.

Mandarin Cauliflower and Broccoli Medley

Description

Making your vegetables more interesting, will create a reason for your family to try any new variation. The aroma of this mixture, while stir-frying, will have everyone sitting at the table, ready to enjoy.

Yields: 4 Servings

Ingredients

2 Tablespoons canola oil
½ teaspoon salt
10 mushrooms, sliced lengthwise
1 small onion, minced
1 cup water
1 ½ cups bite-size cauliflower pieces
1 ½ cups bite-size broccoli pieces
½ cup water
2 teaspoons sugar
2 teaspoons cornstarch dissolved in 1 Tablespoon water

Instructions

1. Heat oil and salt in wok.

2. Add mushrooms and onion.

3. Stir-fry for 2 minutes or until tender.

4. Add water and bring to a boil.

5. Cover and steam for 5 minutes.

6. Uncover and add broccoli.

7. Cover and steam for an additional 10 minutes, stirring occasionally.

8. Uncover and add remaining water and sugar.

9. Bring to a simmer and add cornstarch mix.

10. Stir until sauce thickens and all vegetables are well coated.

Stir Fry Chicken and Peaches

Description

A delicate sauce make this stir fry chicken recipe a hit with the family. Low-cal and nutritious, peaches all extra flavor to a classic sweet and sour classic dish.

Yields: 6 to 8 Servings

Ingredients

1 3-pound chicken, cut into 8 pieces
1 teaspoon salt
½ teaspoon poultry seasoning
3 Tablespoons cornstarch
1 cup canola oil plus 1 Tablespoon oil
1 clove garlic, peeled and crushed
8 ounces frozen sliced, unsweetened peaches, thawed
1 Tablespoon sugar
2 Tablespoons lemon juice
½ cup chicken broth
2 teaspoons cornstarch dissolved in 1 Tablespoon water
10 ounces frozen snow peas
3 cups hot cooked rice

Instructions

1. Fill wok half full with water.

2. Place chicken pieces in a shallow baking dish and sprinkle with salt and poultry seasoning.

3. Place dish on a wire rack atop the wok and cover.

4. Cover chicken and turn wok on medium-high.

5. Steam the chicken for 45 minutes.

6. Remove and dry chicken pieces.

7. Rub cornstarch into each chicken piece.

8. Remove water from wok and wipe dry.

9. Add 1 cup canola oil into wok and heat to just under sizzling.

10. Fry chicken pieces in the hot oil, 2 or 3 pieces at a time until lightly browned.

11. Remove to a plate, lined with paper towels.

12. Pour oil out of wok and discard.

13. Add 1 Tablespoon oil to wok, add garlic, and stir-fry until brown.

14. Remove and discard garlic.

15. Add peaches and sugar, snow peas, stirring into the garlic liquid.

16. Stir in lemon juice.

17. Add chicken broth and heat to boiling.

18. Stir in dissolved cornstarch.

19. Add snow peas, stirring into the liquid.

20. Cover and steam for 30 seconds.

21. Add chicken pieces to wok and cover.

22. Steam for 30 seconds or until chicken is heated.

Serve over hot cooked rice.

Oriental Rice

Description

It seems that every time you have a Chinese-type of meal, there is tons of white rice left over. Put it to good use with this tasty oriental rice recipe. It will make a great side dish for a lunch or dinner menu
Yields: 4 to 6 Serving

Ingredients

1 Tablespoon oil
2 cups cold cooked rice
½ cup chopped water chestnuts
½ cup raisins
¼ cup soy sauce

Instructions

1. Heat oil in wok.

2. Add rice and cook, stirring until coated with oil.

3. Add water chestnuts and raisins.

4. Stir-fry until all is heated.

5. Add soy sauce and blend well.

6. Turn into a serving bowl.

Small portions of leftover meat can also be used for additional flavor.

Sweet and Sour Shrimp

Description

Who doesn't love the awesome flavor of sweet and sour sauce, mixed with shrimp and fresh vegetables. Here is a recipe that will amaze your taste buds and satisfy your hunger.

Yields: 4 Servings

Ingredients

1 carrot, peeled and diagonally sliced
1 green pepper, cut into 1-inch squares
2 cups canola oil
½ teaspoon salt
8 ounces breaded, frozen shrimp
1 clove garlic, peeled and flattened
1 cup unsweetened pineapple chunks, drained (save the juice)
¾ cup mixed sweet pickles, drained

Sauce Ingredients

1 ¼ cup unsweetened pineapple juice
¼ cup white wine vinegar

1 Tablespoon soy sauce
1/3 cup brown sugar
1/4 cup catsup
2 Tablespoons cornstarch

Instructions

Prepare the Sweet and Sour Sauce first.

1. In a small saucepan, combine 1 cup pineapple juice, vinegar, soy sauce, sugar and catsup.

2. Stir over medium heat until simmering.

3. Dissolve cornstarch in ¼ cup pineapple juice and add to pan.

4. Stir until smooth.

5. Remove from heat and set aside.

Stir-Fry Section
1. Place carrot slices in saucepan and cover with water.

2. Boil for 5 minutes
3. Add green pepper and boil for another 5 minutes.

4. Drain and set aside.

5. Add oil and salt to wok.

6. Heat to 375 degrees F.

7. Fry the frozen shrimp, a few at a time, until lightly browned.

8. Drain on paper towels.

9. Remove oil from wok and wipe clean with paper towels.

10. Discard oil.

11. Add 1 Tablespoon oil to wok.

12. Set to high heat.

13. Add garlic, rubbing against sides and bottom until lightly browned.

14. Remove and discard.

15. Add peppers and carrots.

16. Stir-fry for 30 seconds.

17. Add the sweet and sour sauce.

18. Next, add the pineapple chunks and pickles.

19. Stir-fry until hot.

20. Add cooked shrimp and cover all with sauce.

21. Spoon over hot cooked rice.

Pears Cardinal

Description

No one will find these pears boring with the succulent flavor of raspberries, surrounding them. Easy to make while you have your wok out, or use your stove top. Attractive, rich and melt-in-your mouth consistency, make this dessert a great finish to any meal.

Yields: 8 to 10 Servings

Ingredients

6 ripe pears
Red food coloring
20 ounces frozen raspberries, thawed (or fresh is even better)
2 Tablespoons sugar
2 teaspoons cornstarch, dissolved in 2 Tablespoons water
¼ cup kirsch liqueur, or raspberry flavored syrup

Instructions

1. Place a rack in wok that is filled with simmering water.

2. Stand up pears on the rack and cover.

3. Steam for 10 to 15 minutes.

4. Remove pears from rack.

5. Run under cold water to gently remove skin.

6. Rub each pear with a little red food coloring for a blushed appearance.

7. Refrigerate until chilled.

8. Blend raspberries in a blender.

9. Strain out seeds.

10. Place the raspberry puree in a saucepan and bring to a boil.

11. Stir in sugar and dissolved cornstarch.

12. Keep stirring until mixture thickens.

13. Remove from heat and add liqueur or flavored syrup.

14. Refrigerate until well chilled.

15. When ready to serve, place on pear in a serving dish and spoon the sauce over the top.

Chapter 10: List of Low-Carb Foods

Trying to keep all of the terms straight, like carbohydrates, calories, low-fat, and induction, can be difficult to understand. Not all low-carb foods are low-fat, or low in calories. Start with this list of foods that can keep anyone on the straight and narrow in beginning a low-carb diet. After a while, you will learn, just by tasting, how some foods dull your palate in enjoying the rich flavor of natural foods. One of these is sugar. It is a known fact that refined sugar decreases your ability to savor flavor. By ridding your diet of refined sugar, bleached white flour, margarine, and other processed, synthetic additives, you will begin to enjoy the wholesome flavor that low-carb natural foods have to offer.

- Cucumbers
- Broccoli
- Iceberg Lettuce
- Celery
- White Mushrooms
- Turnips
- Radishes
- Romaine Lettuce

- Asparagus
- Green Pepper
- Okra
- Cauliflower
- Cabbage
- Red Bell Pepper
- Spinach
- Beets
- Green Beans
- Carrots
- Kale
- Sugar Snap Peas
- Corn
- Onions
- Watermelon
- Strawberries
- Cantaloupe
- Avocado
- Blackberries
- Honeydew Melon
- Grapefruit
- Oranges
- Peaches
- Papaya
- Cranberries
- Plums
- Raspberries
- Pineapple
- Nectarine
- Blueberries

- Apples
- Pears
- Kiwi Fruit
- Cherries
- Tangerines
- Mango

If you feel that you just can't stay away from refined sugar, try these natural alternatives in cooking and see how quickly your habit begins to fade.

- Molasses
- Sorghum
- Real Maple Syrup
- Maple Sugar
- Sucanat or Rapadura
- Agave Syrup
- Coconut Sugar
- Honey

Bread is a real obstacle for many that have grown up on products made from white flour. If you are able to find bread products with any of the following main ingredients, you will be doing your body a favor.

- Corn
- Soybeans
- Oat Bran
- Barley

- Organic Sprouted Wheat
- Millet

Pasta has grown popular in making quick meals but the ingredients can be full of carbs. While many companies are slow to transform a popular-selling product into one that offers good nutrition, one company is gaining ground because of the low-carb content. Known as Shirataki, the starch is made from the root of devil's tongue, a type of yam. While you will probably never find this product in your local grocery store, keep your eyes open for new types of pasta alternatives in the foreign cuisine section.

Chapter 11: Tips for Prepping

People raised in countries, outside of the United States, are constantly amazed at how our grocery shopping is done. They are used to shopping for fresh produce and seafood on a daily basis, not weekly, as is practiced in the states. How can anything be fresh when it is allowed to set for a week?

To say that it is simple to eat healthier on a low carb diet, according to American standards, would be misleading. Manufacturers of ready-made food stuffs , count on the fact that there is too little time to spend on healthy eating. Popping a cardboard box into the microwave or opening a can, has replaced wholesome foods with convenience. Unfortunately, this way of thinking has led us to where we are today. Weight gain, inadequate vitamin supply, and slow metabolism, is the result of pumping your body with preservatives and sugars that prevent a healthy system. While time is on everyone's mind, there are some short cuts that you can take to prepare for low carb meals.

Freeze, Freeze, Freeze

In the summer, fresh vegetables are everywhere. But

when winter sets in, finding produce can make your search for fresh foods, a real chore. This year, snap up those great looking veggies and freeze so you will have plenty on hand during the winter months.

Not all vegetables freeze well. Those with a high water content can become mushy and less flavorful, like onions and cucumbers. But many other types can retain their shape, presence and vitamins, for meal prepping. Here are some examples of vegetables that can be frozen and ready to use:

- Asparagus
- Beans
- Broccoli
- Cauliflower
- Squash and Zucchini
- Eggplant
- Snow Peas

How to Properly Freeze:

It is not difficult to prepare vegetables for future use, but it does take a little bit of planning. Pick a day for putting up your family's favorite veggies and follow these simple instructions to make an ample supply.

Supplies needed:

- 3-quart Saucepan
- Wire Basket
- Jelly roll pan
- Waxed paper
- Freezer Bags
- Marking Pen

Instructions for Blanching

Select your veggies and prepare by cleaning, cutting and making meal ready.

Fill the saucepan half full of water and bring to a boil.

Put the prepared veggies into the wire basket and plunge into the boiling water for 3 minutes.

Remove and drain. Pat dry to remove any excess water.

Line the jelly roll pan with waxed paper and lay out your vegetables in single file.

Place the jelly roll pan in the freezer, just long enough for the food to freeze.

Remove and place in freezer bags, squeezing out as

much excess water, as possible.

Mark and date each bag and return to the freezer.

By getting into the habit of preparing garden fresh vegetables for future use, you can rest assured that your family will receive no preservatives or additives from packaged foods.

10 Tips for Staying on a Low-Cal Plan

No one claims that it is easy to break bad habits, but if you look at where you are, and where you want to be, anything is possible. Remember when you thought that using a cell phone was the most impossible thing you had ever done? But now you probably wonder how you ever lived without it. Everyone dislikes change but when the future turns out for the better, you wonder how you ever thought differently. Try some of these tips and you will soon be forgetting about those bad eating habits.

1. Use coconut as a sweetener. Why is coconut downplayed so much? It is a wonderful, sweet and tasty type of low-carb accessory that can become irreplaceable. Use it in main dish recipes, savor the juice and discover that it is very addicting.

2. Who started the rumor that eggs were bad? Eggs are a great source of protein and can be eaten alone or used in salads and meals. They are also very portable for a quick energy boost. Use to make sauces, to add texture to foods, or just as a snack in the middle of the day.

3. Never throw leftovers away. You just spent a lot of time on a low-cal meal for your family and believe it or not, you have some scraps to deal with. You already know how good they are for you so wrap them up and use on a salad for lunch tomorrow.

4. Herbs are better than salt. We all have the habit of salting everything that is set in front of us. Break this habit by keeping a variety of herbs close by. The selection will be interesting and fun, plus a lot better than salt, which does nothing but harm your body.

5. Rice is a great filler but not the best when it comes to nutrition. Try something different, like ground cauliflower. The taste will not be so ho-hum and you might just trick your brain into thinking that it is rice, but somehow, even better.

6. Make good use of your muffin pan. Part of the problem with staying on a low- carb diet menu, is thinking that you are going to starve. The portions seem

so tiny and your mind just cannot grab hold of the fact that you will ever be satisfied. Start using a muffin pan to fill with portions so you will get used to having enough. Start with something filling, like pudding or chicken salad. You will be surprised just how much a muffin cup can hold.

7. Salads can be the spice of life. How many other foods are so flexible to accept fruit, meat, and vegetables, without ruining the taste? In addition, dressings and sauces can be an endless supply of flavor. From cheeses to herbs, lemons and limes, you can transform a salad into any flavor you desire.

8. Think of a lettuce leaf as a piece of bread and the need to be fulfilled with a sandwich, will slowly fade away. Wraps are becoming popular with anything and everything. Meat, cheese, pickles, or a mixture of favorite foods. Iceberg lettuce has big meaty leaves for wrapping up tuna salad, eggs, chicken breast, and more.

9. Go on an adventure to an Asian store and look at the labels of pasta. You will probably see some words that are foreign to you, but more than likely, they represent roots and vegetables instead of chemical additives that you do recognize. Asians are not big on bread and grains that make them feel sluggish. Ask someone in the

market about the ingredients, or write down the names and search for yourself.

10. If sweets are your downfall, don't deprive yourself and make the craving worse. Enjoy some chocolate or puddings that can be found on a low carb diet food list. Make ahead to keep on hand for when that craving hits.

Deciding to go on a low-carb diet is not just a choice for losing weight, but changing the way that you look at food. Our society has become accustomed to eating anything that announces 'low-fat' or 'low-carb, that we have been brainwashed into accepting almost anything. Always shop for fresh, or frozen, and learn to enjoy the taste of food that has been replaced with high fat and glucose filled preservatives. Not only will you feel better, but your weight will automatically begin to burn off and give you more energy.

Section 2: Grain Free Cooking

Grain free eating can be hard to think about in a culture that uses flour, corn and other refined starches in almost every food. For some of us, however, grains aren't the healthiest option. Mounting evidence suggests that heavy carbohydrate consumption simply isn't ideal for a significant portion of the population. If you're among these people, you're better off choosing a protein-heavy diet that helps you keep your blood sugar consistent and reduces your risk of diabetes and similar conditions.

For others, the gluten found in a wide variety of grains like wheat, rye and some oats can cause serious digestive and metabolic problems. Whether you have a grain allergy or you suffer from gluten intolerances such as celiac disease, your body simply can't digest grains properly. In severe cases, the nutritional deficiencies caused by this problem can lead to fuzzy thinking, deterioration of the bones and teeth, and even serious mood disorders. The solution is simple: just discontinue grains.

Last but not least, you may wish to avoid grains if you're following a paleo-style diet. These eating plans focus on the foods that were available to our ancestors before the advent of agriculture. That means that grains were consumed infrequently at best, and they were never processed into flour or other highly refined products. The diet relies much more heavily on fresh fruits, vegetables, tubers and animal products such as meat. If you follow a paleo diet, you'll find plenty of material here to keep your taste buds happy and your body healthy.

The Problem of Grains

Grains such as wheat, rice, corn, barley and rye have been an essential part of human diets all over the world since the invention of agriculture. They are appealing, easy to produce in large quantities, and simple to cook. Unfortunately, they aren't necessarily the ideal option for many people. Modern varieties of grains may be especially prone to problems. They have been modified extensively from their ancestral form, containing far more starch and less fiber than their ancestors. In many cases, they seem to be more likely to cause metabolic diseases, intolerances and other problems than even the grains that were available just a century ago.

The problem becomes even more serious when genetically-modified foods appear on the scene. While the basic mechanism of genetic modification is the same whether the process occurs in the field through breeding or in a lab, modern science makes gene tinkering extremely easy. We don't know whether this process has any significant side effects, however. Since many of the grains currently on the market have been genetically modified, it can be hard to tell whether they're having an effect on your health.

These issues are part of why so many people are choosing to limit or eliminate grains in their diet. While grain free dieting isn't for everyone, a significant percentage of the people who try it find themselves feeling stronger, more energetic and healthier. Headaches, excess weight gain and even some long-lasting health problems decrease and even vanish in many people. In many cases, it seems as though our bodies simply aren't meant to use grains in the forms that are currently available.

Transitioning to a Grain Free Diet

If you have reason to believe that you could benefit from a grain free diet, you may still have trouble making the leap. After all, most cultures still have a basic diet that is built on one or more grains. Whether it's the ubiquitous bread found in North American and European cooking, the corn we see in so much native and Central American cuisine, or the rice found throughout Asia, grains seem to be everywhere. By choosing to eliminate them from your diet, you have to deliberately go against the flow. Many people who are seeking to cut out excess grain consumption have run into trouble finding good, healthy recipes to help them.

The key is to approach the process carefully and with a well-defined plan. If you're hoping to cut your carbohydrates or want to use a paleo-inspired diet plan, you may want to slowly substitute more grain free foods in your diet. Over time, you can replace your favorites with foods that are just as delicious, without seriously disrupting your life.

For others this method won't work as well. This is the

case if you know you have a serious allergy or intolerance to one or more grains. You may also have trouble with the slow substitution technique if you are using specific kinds of low carbohydrate diets. In these cases, you'll need to start over from scratch. Remove all the grain based foods from your home and avoid picking up new ones to reduce temptation.

No matter how you make the transition, it's important to have a plan. Haphazardly trying to start on a new way of eating is one of the surest ways to guarantee the failure of this lifestyle change. Instead, make sure you have a good idea of what's available to you in your new, grain-free lifestyle, and choose the most appealing foods you possibly can. It's much easier to make the switch when you know that you have something to look forward to.

A Question of Nutritional Balance

If you're like many people, you're probably used to getting the bulk of your nutrition from grain-based foods such as bread or pasta. That can make transitioning to a diet that's lower in or completely free of grains a little daunting. After all, no one wants to discover that they've been eating a nutritionally imbalanced diet after making this kind of change, and many government health organizations recommend eating up to 11 servings of grains every day.

In reality, consuming this many grain-based products isn't necessary for good health. Many cultures consume far less, basing their diets on non-grain starches, fresh fruits and vegetables, and healthy meats with no significant health issues. As long as you pay attention to the basic recommendations of your specific grain-free diet plan or your nutritionist, you shouldn't have too many problems with balance. Focus on eating a variety of different foods instead of just the same few every day, and you'll soon be feeling healthier and happier than you ever did while consuming lots of processed grains.

Grain Free Shopping and Cooking Tips

Shopping for grain-free foods can be extremely difficult, especially if you're used to consuming a lot of convenience foods. That's because many apparently non-grain products actually contain extremely processed grain ingredients. For instance, many ketchups, pasta sauces and even commercial French fries have been treated with dextrose, glucose and maltodextrin. These sweeteners are derived from corn or rice, and they can be incompatible with a non-grain diet.

You may also find grains in non-dairy milks, baking powder, spice mixes, flavored beverages and many other foods. If you choose any kind of prepared meat, such as pre-made hamburger patties, there is a good chance that a corn, wheat, or rice-based thickener and binder has been used in its preparation. Even soy sauce usually contains hidden wheat unless otherwise labeled. Read packages carefully and avoid any product that contains thickeners, malt ingredients, dextrose and similar sweeteners, non-specific starches such as modified food starch, or ingredients labeled simply as "vegetable" or "plant" proteins.

It's also important to be careful in the kitchen, especially if you suffer from an allergy or intolerance. In shared cooking spaces, it's very easy for grains from a roommate or family member's cooking to end up in your food. Wash all knives, cutting boards, counters and containers carefully before using them to reduce the risk of contamination. While this may not be a concern for everyone, in some cases even a small amount of a grain-based product can make you very sick.

Reading the Recipe Key

Since there are so many reasons to seek out grain free recipes, not every meal will be right for every kind of diet. This book uses the symbols GF, P and LC to mark gluten-free, paleo and low carbohydrate recipes to ensure that you can quickly and easily find the perfect dish for your next meal. While most recipes will meet the requirements of more than one type of diet, it's important to check before you start cooking if you want to ensure perfect nutrition for your dietary requirements.

Breakfast

No-Grain Granola (GF, P, LC)

Breakfast cereal is an important part of many people's regular daily routine, but it can be hard to have cereal without grains. This no-grain granola recipe relies on fresh raw nuts and seeds rather than oats or wheat. It's sweetened naturally with dates and uses no oil, so it's suitable for all kinds of low-carbohydrate diets. You'll enjoy this rich, delicious and very natural breakfast option, whether you have it with fresh fruit and your favorite dairy or plant milk or you eat it on its own. To increase the sweetness, just add more date paste.

Ingredients

2 cups raw pecans
2 cups raw cashews or Brazil nuts
2 cups raw pumpkin or sunflower seeds
1 cup plain coconut flakes
1 cup dates
1 cup water
½ cup flax seeds
1 vanilla bean or 2 teaspoons vanilla extract
½ teaspoon cinnamon or mixed sweet spices

Place the whole nuts and seeds in a large bowl and cover them with lukewarm water, stirring to combine. Allow to rest at room temperature for 8 hours to 2 days. This process sprouts the seeds and removes phytic acid, which can cause digestive problems. In a food processor or blender, combine the dates and 1 cup of warm to hot water. Process for about 1 minute, or until a smooth paste is formed. Split the vanilla bean and scrape out the contents.

Drain the nuts and seeds, then add the coconut flakes, flax seeds, vanilla, date paste, vanilla scrapings and cinnamon. Stir to combine. Line a baking sheet with parchment paper and pour the granola mixture out onto it, spreading into an even layer. Dehydrate in 170 degree Fahrenheit oven for about 8 hours or until the granola is crunchy. Stir periodically to break up clumps. Allow to cool and place in an airtight container for storage. This mixture lasts for 3 to 4 weeks at room temperature.

Fresh Homestyle Beef Sausages (GF, P, LC)

Most commercial sausage recipes rely on grains as fillers and binders for the meat. This makes the sausage easier to prepare and protects the manufacturer's bottom line, but it can be disaster for your grain-free diet. Making your own sausage at home is a surprisingly simple way to enjoy this classic breakfast meat without worrying about the inclusion of oatmeal, wheat, pork or other undesirable substances. For a different flavor, substitute chicken.

Ingredients

2 pounds grass-fed boneless chuck steak
1 tablespoon fresh thyme
1 tablespoon fresh sage
¾ tablespoon coarse salt
½ teaspoon red pepper or sharp paprika

Trim the fat from the meat and discard, then chop the beef into cubes approximately 1 inch across. Freeze on a baking sheet for about 20 minutes, or until the texture is relatively firm. Combine the herbs, pepper or paprika and salt in a small bowl. Remove the meat from the freezer. Place ½ of it in the refrigerator and place the other half in the bowl of a powerful food processor.

Sprinkle with about ½ of the spice mixture and pulse until the meat is in very small pieces and the spices are well incorporated throughout.

Spread a piece of parchment paper on a counter or cutting board and transfer the meat to the center of the paper. Roll the paper around the meat to form a log, twisting the ends to secure them or using a rubber band. Repeat the process with the remaining meat and spices to form two fat sausages. Freeze for 30 minutes before cooking to make the slicing process easier. Cook in ¼ inch thick slices over medium-high heat and serve with eggs, sauces, soup or on pizzas. This recipe can be frozen for up to 2 months without loss of flavor.

Almond Cottage Cheese Pancakes (GF, P*, LC**)

Pancakes and other breakfast sweets can be hard to come by when you're on a grain-free diet, but that doesn't mean you have to give them up completely. This recipe uses starches derived from tubers, not grains, along with flour from nuts and seeds. If you've been missing that classic pancake breakfast, this is the recipe for you.

Ingredients

½ cup almond flour
½ cup cottage cheese
3 large eggs
1/8 cup coconut flour
1 tablespoon raw honey
3/8 teaspoon baking powder
¼ teaspoon cream of tartar or lemon juice
¼ teaspoon plain gelatin granules
¼ teaspoon vanilla extract
salt to taste
2 tablespoons coconut oil

Place the almond flour, cottage cheese, eggs, coconut flour, honey, baking powder, cream of tartar, gelatin, vanilla and salt in a food processor or blender and process until combined and completely smooth. Heat 1 tablespoon of coconut oil in a heavy-bottomed skillet or griddle to medium-high. Spoon the batter into the pan in a thin layer about 4 inches across and cook until the bottom is golden and the top looks relatively dry. Flip and cook until the other side has browned. Remove the cakes from the pan and repeat until all batter has been consumed. Serve with fruit, yogurt, honey, syrup or jam.

* This recipe is not suitable for paleo dieters who avoid dairy products or eggs.

** To make this recipe low-carbohydrate friendly, omit the honey or substitute a no-calorie liquid sweetener according to package instructions.

Open-faced Apple, Egg and Salmon Sandwich (GF, P, LC)

This breakfast recipe combines the richness of egg with the sharp sweetness of a tart baking apple and the salty savor of salmon. Look for organic apples whenever possible. This recipe makes four sandwiches, but it's easy to cut back to serve just one or two.

6 large eggs
4 slices smoked salmon
2 large tart baking apples, such as Granny Smith
2 tablespoons coconut oil
salt and pepper to taste
Romano cheese (optional)

Crack the eggs into a medium bowl and beat until thick and creamy. Season with salt and pepper. In a medium pan, heat the coconut oil to medium-low. Pour in the eggs and allow to set, then scramble, cooking for about 5 minutes. Remove from heat. Core the apples and slice each one in half. Place the apple halves cut-side-up in an oven-safe baking dish. Top each piece of apple with a slice of salmon and ¼ of the scrambled eggs. Garnish with thinly-shaved Romano cheese if desired. Bake at 400 degrees Fahrenheit for 10 minutes, or until apples are warm throughout.

Almond Waffles (GF, P*)

Using almond flour produces a crunchy waffle that makes an excellent snack. Make sure that you preheat the waffle iron for at least 15 minutes before cooking this recipe, since a cold iron can result in trouble removing the finished waffles. Serve with fresh fruit, coconut oil or butter, cream or maple syrup.

Ingredients

2 ¾ cup almond flour
2 ¾ cups tapioca flour
2 3/4 cups water
1/4 teaspoon salt
1 tablespoon coconut oil

Brush the waffle iron with coconut oil and preheat. Combine the almond flour, tapioca flour and salt in a large bowl. Add the oil and water, stirring vigorously until well combined. Allow the batter to stand for five minutes, then remix before pouring the individual waffles. Pour about 1 ½ cups of batter into the waffle iron at a time and cook on high heat for 15 minutes or until the surface is crisp and golden. Reheat the waffle iron and re-stir the batter before cooking each set of waffles.

* Some paleo diets permit the use of starch from tubers such as tapioca or arrowroot, but this may not apply to all cases.

Green Eggs (GF, P, LC)

With or without the addition of your favorite non-pork "ham," this recipe will definitely turn heads and please your taste buds. The addition of flavorful, nutrient-dense fresh kale makes simple scrambled eggs bright green and highly unusual. For a change, consider substituting parsley or spinach instead of the kale.

Ingredients

4 large eggs
½ pound kale
coconut oil for frying
salt and black pepper to taste

Remove the ribs and stems from the kale and discard. Combine the remaining leaves with the eggs, salt and pepper in a blender and process until completely smooth. Heat the oil to high in a large skillet. Pour the egg mixture into the pan and allow it to set, then scramble gently with a silicone spatula or wooden spoon until creamy and cooked through. Serve with breakfast sausage or your favorite non-grain bread.

Hot Porridge (GF, P, LC)

Hot porridges such as oatmeal may not be romantic, but many people find that they miss these foods' simple appeal when it's time to give up grains. This comforting version is based on nuts and seeds, but it still has that creamy texture. For a savory version, substitute black pepper for the cinnamon and serve with butter, paprika, cheese or even crispy bits of turkey bacon.

Ingredients

1 cup water
¼ cup chopped walnuts
2 tablespoons plain shredded coconut
1 tablespoon pumpkin or sunflower seeds
1 tablespoon chia seeds
1 tablespoon flax seeds
1 teaspoon cinnamon
¼ teaspoon salt

Bring the water to a boil. Combine all the other ingredients in a powerful blender and process until a fine meal is produced. Pour the boiling water over the entire mixture and cover. Blend slowly, increasing the intensity, until the porridge is smooth and creamy. Serve hot, with dried fruit, cream, honey or milk.

No-Grain Breakfast Burritos (GF, P, LC)

Breakfast burritos are a tasty and convenient way to enjoy a savory start to your day. When corn and wheat tortillas are no longer an option, we turn to egg tortillas instead. Filled with taco meat, guacamole and other tasty ingredients, this also makes an excellent light lunch.

Ingredients

1 pound ground turkey
2 ripe avocados
1 small red onion
1 medium tomato
1 lime
2 cloves garlic
2 tablespoons cilantro
1 teaspoon salt
1 tablespoon grain-free taco seasoning
12 eggs
1 tablespoon grain-free hot sauce
1 tablespoon coconut oil.

In a skillet over medium heat, brown the turkey. Sprinkle the meat with 1 tablespoon of taco seasoning, stirring to combine. Remove from heat. Mash the avocados, chop the onion, tomato, cilantro and garlic, and combine in a small bowl. Season with salt and lime juice, mixing until you have achieved your preferred consistency.

In a separate skillet, heat the coconut oil to medium-low. Beat two eggs until creamy and thick. Season with salt and hot sauce, then pour a thin layer into the hot skillet. Allow to cook all the way through on one side and remove to a plate. Repeat the process until you have 12 egg tortillas. To serve, top each tortilla with a spoonful of taco meat and guacamole. Garnish with green onions or sour cream if desired.

Sweet Potato Breakfast Casserole (GF, P, LC)

This quiche-like dish uses grated sweet potatoes to produce an appealing and grain-free crust, into which are piled eggs, meat, cheese and fresh herbs. Substitute your favorites to produce variations on this exciting brunch casserole. This dish is great hot and fresh out of the oven, but it can also be served cold for lunch or a snack.

Ingredients

2 medium sweet potatoes
4 eggs
¾ cup diced turkey or your favorite breakfast sausage
2 tablespoons coconut oil
1 small onion
1 tablespoon fresh basil
1 tablespoon fresh oregano
1 tablespoon flat-leaf parsley
Salt to taste
½ cup cheddar cheese (optional)

Grate the sweet potatoes finely. Grease a pie plate using 1 teaspoon of coconut oil. Salt the sweet potatoes and press them evenly over the sides and bottom of the pan. Melt the coconut oil and pour it over the layered sweet potatoes. Bake in a 425 degree Fahrenheit oven for 20 minutes, or until crisp but not burnt. Remove and allow to cool slightly.

Spread turkey or sausage in an even layer over the bottom of the crust. Sprinkle cheese over the meat. In a small bowl, beat the eggs thoroughly. Chop the herbs and add them to the eggs. Season with salt to taste and pour over the meat and cheese. Reduce the oven temperature to 350 degrees and bake for 30 minutes or until the center is solid. Allow to set slightly, slice and serve.

Main Dishes

Pot Roast with Fresh Vegetables (GF, P, LC)

A traditional pot roast makes a great addition to almost any grain-free dinner. About half the fat in the beef is monounsaturated, or "good" fat. Plus, this meat is full of vitamin B12 and other essential nutrients. When combined with mustard, garlic and other delicious spices, it's an easy and appealing choice for just about any meal. It also freezes well, making this roast a good option for single-serving meals later.

Ingredients

5 pounds chuck roast
2 pounds mushrooms
2 large onions
1 ½ pounds carrots
4 cups butternut squash
2 cups beef broth
2 tablespoons tomato paste
2 tablespoons sunflower oil
1 small head garlic
1 tablespoon thyme
1 tablespoon sharp paprika

1 teaspoon salt
1 teaspoon black pepper
2 bay leaves

Trim the excess fat from the roast. In a small bowl, combine the salt, mustard, thyme, pepper and paprika. Rub this mixture over the outside of the roast. Heat the oil in a large Dutch oven to medium-high. Place the roast inside and brown on all sides, turning periodically. Peel and coarsely chop the onions and garlic. Add these to the pot along with the stock and tomato paste. Bring all to a simmer and cover, cooking for about 10 minutes.

Remove from heat and place the entire pot in the oven. Bake at 325 degrees Fahrenheit for 3 hours. Coarsely chop the mushrooms, carrots and squash. Remove the roast and add the vegetables, then recover and bake for an additional hour. Serve immediately right from the pot.

Tropical Tilapia (GF, P)

Once unknown, tilapia has become one of the most common whitefish options. This species has tender flesh with a mild flavor, plus it's harvested from fish that repopulate readily and live in a wide range of environments. That makes it a better choice than many traditional whitefish, whose numbers are on the decline. Originally from tropical habitats, tilapia taste delicious when combined with other hot-climate foods such as pineapple, coconut and sweet potatoes.

Ingredients

1 pound tilapia fillets
2 large sweet potatoes
1 large onion
2 cups coconut milk
1 tablespoon coconut oil
¼ cup fresh pineapple
salt and black pepper to taste

Bake, boil or steam the sweet potatoes until they are tender and remove the skins. Slice them into thick rounds. Heat a tablespoon of coconut oil in a large frying pan over medium heat. Dice the onions and cook them in the oil until they are softened and translucent, but not brown. Stir the coconut milk to emulsify any solids and add it directly to the onions. Bring to a simmer, then add the tilapia fillets in a single layer. Cook the fish in the coconut milk mixture for about 5 minutes or until the bottom side is opaque. Flip the fillets and add the pineapple in a single layer on top. Cook the entire pan for an additional five minutes, then serve on top of the sweet potato rounds. Drizzle the remaining coconut milk and onion mixture on top of the dish and season with salt and pepper.

Barbecue Chicken with Grain-free Sauce (GF, P)

Barbecue lovers are often disappointed when they go grain free, since most commercial barbecue sauce is chock full of **Ingredients**
 derived from wheat, rice and corn. Fortunately, it's extremely easy to make your own delicious barbecue sauce at home. These very simple chicken wings are excellent hot or cold, and they make the perfect addition to just about any cookout.

20 chicken wings
1 cup tomato sauce
1 large juice orange
3 shallots
½ cup honey
¼ cup vinegar
2 cloves garlic
1-inch piece ginger
1 teaspoon fresh thyme
1 teaspoon salt
½ teaspoon sharp paprika

Dice the shallots, garlic and ginger finely. Combine with all ingredients other than chicken wings in a medium-sized pan and simmer over medium-low heat until the onions are soft, or about 45 minutes. Allow to cool.

Wash the chicken wings and remove the tips. In a large bowl, toss the wings with ½ cup of barbecue sauce. Place them in a 9 x 13 inch casserole pan and bake at 350 degrees Fahrenheit for 30 to 45 minutes. Use the shorter time period if you intend to finish the wings on a charcoal or gas grill. Otherwise, finish by turning the oven to broil and cook for approximately 10 minutes, or until wings are properly browned. Transfer to a large bowl and toss with another ½ cup barbecue sauce, then serve.

Zucchini Pasta with Roasted Sweet Potatoes and Coconut Pesto (GF, P)

While meat makes up a big part of most grain-free diets, that doesn't mean it has to appear in every meal. This pasta-style squash dish is light and delicious, with a rich pesto-based sauce and plenty of protein from coconut. It also includes sweet potatoes to help ensure that it's filling as well as tasty. Unlike many of the recipes in this book, this zucchini pasta is best eaten fresh and does not store well.

Ingredients

2 large zucchinis
2 medium sweet potatoes
1 cup mixed greens
1 cup fresh basil
½ cup plain shredded coconut
½ cup hot water
¼ cup olive oil
1 lemon
salt and black pepper to taste

Cut the zucchini into long ribbons using a spiral slicer or a paring knife. Chop the sweet potatoes into large pieces and toss with 1 tablespoon olive oil. Place in an oven-safe dish and roast at 375 degrees until tender. Set aside and allow to cool. Bring a pot of water to a boil over medium-high heat and add the zucchini. Cook for 2 to 3 minutes, or until zucchini is translucent but not mushy. Remove from water and plunge immediately into a bowl of ice water. Drain and set aside.

Juice the lemon. Combine in a blender or food processor with coconut, hot water, olive oil and basil. Season with salt and pepper to taste. Process until smooth and toss with finished zucchini pasta. Serve over salad greens, topped with sweet potatoes.

American Taco Pie (GF, P, LC)

This Americanized Mexican dish is hearty and savory. It also freezes well in individual portions, making it an excellent choice for lunches or dinners on the go. Choose relatively lean ground beef, grass-fed if possible, for the best flavor.

Ingredients

1 ½ cups almond flour
¼ cup coconut oil
1 teaspoon salt
1 pound ground beef
1 tablespoon olive oil
1 medium onion
1 sweet red bell pepper
1 avocado
2 tablespoons grain-free taco seasoning
salt and pepper to taste

In a large bowl, mix the salt, coconut oil and almond flour, blending until a moldable dough forms. Transfer this dough to a standard pie plate and press into an even layer over the whole surface. In a large skillet, heat the olive oil to medium-high. Chop the onions and cook until softened and translucent. Add the ground beef and brown until completely cooked. Mix in the taco seasoning, salt and pepper. Cook for an addition two minutes and remove from heat. Pour the beef mixture into the pie plate and bake for 30 minutes at 350 degrees Fahrenheit, or until the crust is firm. Chop the lettuce, pepper and avocado roughly. Top the finished pie with vegetables and serve immediately.

Braised Chicken with Sweet Potatoes and Fennel Bulb (GF, P)

Chicken legs are inexpensive and flavorful, especially when combined with vitamin A-rich sweet potatoes and the unique taste of fennel. Don't be afraid of the amount of lemon juice required in this recipe; it helps brighten all the other tastes and adds a delightful natural tang that you shouldn't miss. For an extra touch, serve the chicken with a small curl of lemon peel as garnish.

4 chicken legs
2 cups chicken broth
3 medium sweet potatoes
1 bulb fennel
4 scallions
1 small head garlic
2 lemons
2 tablespoons coconut oil
salt and pepper to taste

Heat the coconut oil to medium high in a large skillet. Sear the chicken legs for about 5 minutes per side, or until lightly browned. Transfer to a large, oven-safe pot. Thinly slice the fennel and scallions. Mince the garlic and roughly chop the sweet potatoes. Reheat the skillet and add the fennel, cooking for about 5 minutes, or until the fennel is golden brown. Add the garlic and green onions, reduce heat, and cook for an additional 3 minutes or until the onions are wilted. Transfer the contents of the pan to the pot with the chicken. Juice the lemons and add the juice to the pot, along with the stock, salt and pepper. Cover and bake for 40 minutes at 300 degrees Fahrenheit, or until the chicken is cooked through and the sweet potatoes are tender.

Baked Cashew Chicken (GF, P, LC)

This Asian-inspired main dish is rich, sweet and flavorful. It also provides plenty of manganese, magnesium and copper, essential nutrients that many people lack. This meal is great if you need extra energy or you're cooking for a big group. Because of the fat in the cashews and coconut milk, this dish may separate when chilled. Just warm it up again and stir to restore the texture.

Ingredients

1 pound boneless, skinless chicken breast
2 cups water
1 cup cashews
½ cup coconut milk
¼ cup fresh mint
1 medium yellow onion
4 cloves garlic
1 lime
1-inch piece fresh ginger
2 tablespoons coconut oil
1 tablespoon ground coriander
1 tablespoon ground cumin seeds
1 teaspoon cinnamon
1 teaspoon cloves
salt and pepper to taste

Cut the onions into quarters and combine in a food processor with the cashews, ginger and garlic. Process until a soft puree forms and set aside. Heat the coconut oil in a medium pan over medium-high heat. Add the puree and stir-fry for about 5 minutes or until browned. Add the cumin, cloves, cinnamon and coriander and allow to cook for an additional 5 minutes, stirring periodically. Add the coconut milk and water. Season with salt and black pepper according to preference. Place the chicken in an oven-safe casserole dish and pour the coconut milk mixture over the meat. Cook at 300 degrees Fahrenheit for about 30 minutes, or until the chicken is cooked through. Serve with chopped mint and lime slices.

Savory Braised Duck (GF, P, LC)

Most people eat plenty of chicken and turkey, but very little duck. In fact, some have never enjoy this rich, flavorful bird! This simple braised recipe makes it easy to enjoy the nutrient-rich dark meat of this slightly unusual type of poultry. If duck is unavailable, you can substitute chicken thighs or similar cuts, but duck is definitely best. Allow the dish to rest for a little while after cooking to produce the tastiest finished product.

Ingredients

4 duck legs
1 cup duck or chicken stock
1 small head garlic
1 medium onion
1 stalk celery
2 medium carrots
1 ½ pounds tomatoes
1 small head broccoli
2 tablespoons flat-leaf parsley
1 tablespoon duck fat or coconut milk
1 tablespoon fresh thyme
salt and pepper to taste

Heat the duck fat or coconut oil in a large Dutch oven

over medium-high heat. Brown the duck legs, turning several times. Remove and set aside. Dice the garlic, onion, celery, carrots and tomatoes. Reheat the Dutch oven and sauté the vegetables in the remaining fat for about 5 minutes, or until tender. Return the duck legs to the pot and add the stock and thyme. Cook for approximately 90 minutes at about 325 degrees Fahrenheit, or until the carrots are soft and the duck is cooked through. Add the broccoli 15 minutes before the cooking process is done. Allow the meat to rest for 10 minutes, then serve garnished with parsley.

Stuffed Bell Peppers with Veal (GF, P, LC)

Ordinary stuffed peppers rely on conventionally-grown hamburger, but this version uses tender veal for a different taste and texture. To get the best results, look for pastured veal rather than crate-raised, since the texture of the meat is much better. Despite the lack of carbohydrates, this meal is extremely filling. Consider packing an extra pepper or two for lunch the next day!

Ingredients

1 pound ground veal
3 sweet red bell peppers
2 sweet orange bell peppers
3 tablespoons olive oil
1 medium red onion
½ pound cherry tomatoes
1 tablespoon fresh cilantro
1 tablespoon fresh oregano
1 tablespoon fresh marjoram
3 cloves garlic
salt and black pepper to taste

Remove the stems, ribs and seeds from all the bell peppers. Mince one red bell pepper and set aside. Cut the other four peppers in half, wash thoroughly, and arrange on a cooking dish, cut-side up. Brush with 1 tablespoon of olive oil and bake in a 350 degree oven for 20 minutes. Remove and set aside to cool.

In a separate pan, heat the remaining two tablespoons of olive oil to medium-high. Mince the garlic and onions and add to the pan, along with the minced red bell pepper. Saute for 2 minutes or until soft. Add the veal and season to taste using salt and black pepper. Cook, stirring occasionally, until the meat is done through. Add the fresh herbs and cherry tomatoes and continue cooking for an additional 2 minutes.

Stuff each pepper half with the meat mixture. Cover the entire pan with a sheet of aluminum foil or a lid and bake again for 25 minutes. Uncover and finish in the oven for an additional 10 minutes. Serve with a fresh salad.

No-Rice Pad Thai (GF, P, LC)

Pad Thai, the famous stir-fried noodle dish, is traditionally made with highly-refined rice noodles. This version uses mung bean noodles, which lack some of the health problems normally associated with rice. For a version that's lower in carbohydrates, consider substituting Japanese Shirataki noodles, which are made from a yam-like tuber and are about 97 percent water. While the basic recipe is vegetarian, it's easy to add in your favorite meat or seafood for a heartier version.

Ingredients

6 ounces dried mung bean noodles
1 large head broccoli
2 large onion
¼ cup peanuts or cashews
3 tablespoons coconut oil
4 scallions
3 cloves garlic
1 tablespoon sesame oil
1 tablespoon honey
1 teaspoon tamarind paste
1 teaspoon wheat-free tamari or fish sauce

Fill a large pot with water and bring to a boil over high

heat. Cook noodles according to package instructions, drain, and set aside. In a large wok or skillet heat the coconut oil to medium-high. Slice the onion, scallions and garlic. Stir fry the onion until lightly browned. Add the broccoli, breaking it up into individual florets. Stir fry until the broccoli turns bright green and becomes tender. Stir in garlic, followed by noodles. In a small bowl, combine sesame oil, tamarind paste, tamari and honey. Pour this mixture over the noodles and vegetable, stirring vigorously to prevent sticking and burning. Serve on individual plates garnished with scallions and crushed peanuts.

Baking and Desserts

Almond-coconut Chocolate Chip Cookies (GF, P)

Commercial chocolate chip cookies are loaded with preservatives, white flour, processed sugar and fillers. Even the kind you normally make at home require a number of heavily-processed, genetically modified
Ingredients
. Skip those unappealing cookies in favor of this recipe, which relies on natural sugars, almond flour and coconut flour to provide plenty of nutrition without the starch. Stick to store-bought almond flour to ensure proper lightness; the homemade variety can yield a very flat cookie.

Ingredients

5/8 cup almond flour
5 tablespoons unsalted butter
4 ounces grain-free dark chocolate
2 tablespoons honey or maple syrup
1 tablespoon coconut flour
1 large egg
1/3 teaspoon salt
¼ teaspoon vanilla extract

¼ teaspoon plain gelatin granules
¼ teaspoon baking soda

Bring butter to room temperature and combine with honey or syrup in a large bowl. Add gelatin, egg and vanilla. Allow the mixture to rest for 5 minutes. In a separate bowl, combine the almond and coconut flours, salt and baking soda. Add the dry ingredients to the wet mixture slowly, stirring continuously. Beat until combined. Chop chocolate into small pieces and stir into the cookie mixture. Line a baking pan with parchment paper. Scoop by teaspoonful's onto the pan, leaving plenty of space for the cookies to spread. Bake in a 350 degree Fahrenheit oven for 12 minutes, or until the edges brown slightly. Eat warm with a glass of your favorite dairy or plant milk.

Honey-Buttermilk Panna Cotta (GF, P*, LC**)

Traditional panna cotta is naturally grain free, making it a great substitute for commercial puddings laden with corn starch. This version uses buttermilk for extra flavor and natural maple sweeteners. Whenever possible, stick to using real vanilla beans, which provide a more subtle and interesting taste than extracts. Enjoy this rich and appealing recipe with plenty of fresh raspberries or strawberries.

1 ½ cups natural buttermilk
1 cup heavy cream
1/3 cup maple syrup
1 tablespoon warm water
2 ¼ teaspoons plain gelatin granules
1/2 vanilla bean or 1 teaspoon vanilla extract

Combine the gelatin with 1 tablespoon of warm water in a small bowl. Allow to stand for 10 minutes. In a medium saucepan, heat the cream and maple syrup to medium, whisking continuously to prevent curdling. Allow the mixture to steam slightly, then remove from the heat and allow to cool for five minutes. Whisk in the gelatin mixture until all granules have dissolved completely. Slit the vanilla bean and scrape the contents into the gelatin-cream mixture. Add buttermilk, whisking until the mixture is smooth and creamy. Pour into one large pan or six individual bowls. Refrigerate until firm, 6 hours or more.

*The cream and buttermilk make this recipe unsuitable for paleo dieters.

** Replace the maple syrup with your favorite non-caloric sweeteners to reduce the carbohydrate count of this dessert.

No-Grain Sandwich Bread (GF, P, LC)

Going grain-free doesn't mean saying goodbye to sandwiches, French toast, bread pudding or stuffing, as long as you know how to use your ingredients. This bread is gluten free and filled with nutrient-dense foods, so you'll be surprised at how satisfying it can be. Fluffy, nutty and light, this bread is everything you dreamed grain-free eating could be!

Ingredients

1 3/4 cups almond flour
5 eggs
¼ cup flax seed meal
1/8 cup coconut flour
1 ¾ tablespoons coconut oil
1 tablespoon vinegar
1 tablespoon honey or date paste
1 teaspoon baking soda
¼ teaspoon salt

In a large bowl, combine the almond and coconut flours, flax meal, baking soda and salt. In a separate bowl, whisk together the eggs, coconut oil, vinegar and honey. Pour the wet ingredients into the dry mixture, stirring continuously until just combined. Grease a medium loaf pan and pour the batter in, spreading with a spatula if necessary. Bake at 350 degrees Fahrenheit for 30 minutes or until the top of the loaf browns lightly and the center is firm. Allow to cool and serve.

Banana Coconut Muffins (GF, P, LC)

These muffins are a delicious treat after dinner or for a quick breakfast on a workday. Their flavor improves a day or so after baking, so don't be afraid to make extra and store them in your refrigerator. The bananas and dates provide plenty of sweetness, so there's no reason to add more carbohydrate-heavy options. If you are in the very-low-carbohydrate phase of a low carb diet, however, these muffins may not be suitable. Try them with a little coconut oil or softened butter, or eat them on their own.

Ingredients

6 large eggs
3 large bananas
¾ cup coconut flour
½ cup walnuts
5 tablespoons coconut milk
¼ cup coconut oil
2 tablespoons dates
1 tablespoon hot water
2 ½ teaspoons baking powder
½ teaspoon lemon juice
1 teaspoon salt

Soak the dates in the hot water for 10 minutes, then mash with a fork. Combine in a large bowl with the eggs, coconut milk, lemon juice and salt. Stir in coconut oil and set aside. Sift the baking soda and coconut flour into a medium bowl, then stir the dry ingredients slowly into the liquid ones. Mix until no lumps are visible and the ingredients are well mixed.

Peel and mash the bananas, then fold them into the muffin mixture until completely combined. Stir in walnuts. Scoop into a greased 12-cup muffin pan and bake at 400 degrees Fahrenheit for 18 to 20 minutes. Remove from oven and allow to cool for 10 minutes, then release from pan with the tip of a butter knife and enjoy.

No-flour Chocolate Lava Cake (GF, P)

If you're looking for the perfect holiday dessert indulgence without a trace of grains, this chocolate lava cake is the perfect choice. It includes dark chocolate, which is known for its healthy antioxidants, as well as natural sweeteners. To make ahead, follow the recipe recommendations up to the baking step, then freeze the entire tin and bring to room temperature about a half hour before you bake the cake.

Ingredients

½ pound unsweetened baking chocolate
2/3 cup unsalted butter or coconut oil
2/3 cup honey
6 egg yolks
3 egg whites

Combine the chocolate and butter or coconut oil in a heavy-bottomed pot over low heat. In a separate bowl, beat the honey and egg yolks until they are creamy, thick and fluffy. Add the chocolate mixture directly to the egg yolk mixture and beat vigorously for 5 to 10 minutes or until well combined. In a separate container, beat the egg whites until they become frothy and develop stiff peaks. Fold the meringue into the chocolate mixture carefully until just combined. Grease 6 individual ramekins and divide the batter between them. Bake in a 425 degree Fahrenheit oven for 5 to 7 minutes, or until the center is hot and liquid but the edges are solid. Serve hot with your favorite ice cream or frozen yogurt.

Coconut-vanilla Frozen Dessert (GF, P, LC)

If you read the ingredients on your favorite ice cream package, you may be surprised by how many grain products and fillers it includes. Homemade recipes are often grain-free, but they still rely on refined sugars and other ingredients that tend to be unhealthy. This recipe produces a great-tasting frozen dessert you can make at home without an ice cream maker, plus it's low in carbohydrates and paleo diet-friendly!

Ingredients

2 cups coconut milk
2 large eggs
2 vanilla beans or 4 tablespoons vanilla extract
3 tablespoons raw honey or equivalent no-calorie sweetener

Slit the vanilla beans and scrape them thoroughly. Combine the vanilla scrapings with the coconut milk in a double boiler and heat over low heat until steaming. Add the honey or no-calorie sweetener and stir until dissolved. In a separate bowl, whisk the eggs until they are fluffy and thick. Ladle 1/3 to ½ cup of the hot coconut milk mixture into the eggs, whisking vigorously to combine. Repeat the process, then add the egg mixture to the remainder of the coconut milk mixture.

Whisk for 2 to 3 minutes, or until a thick, smooth custard has formed. Remove from heat and allow the custard to cool to room temperature, then transfer to the refrigerator for at least an hour. Pour the custard into a large baking dish and place in the freezer for about 2 hours or until completely set. Stir vigorously to break up the ice once every 15 to 30 minutes. Remove this dessert from the freezer 10 minutes before serving.

Almond Flour Blueberry Muffins (GF, P, LC*)

This classic snack and breakfast favorite is remarkably simple. It substitutes almond flour for the standard white flour, and natural honey for refined sugar. You'll enjoy the traditional taste, smell and texture of these delicious muffins, whether you eat them fresh out of the oven or save a few for snacking. If your diet doesn't permit use of dairy, consider substituting a grain free soy or coconut yogurt instead.

Ingredients

2 ½ cups almond flour
1 cup fresh blueberries
4 tablespoons butter or coconut milk
2 eggs
1/3 cup honey
1/3 cup yogurt
½ vanilla bean or 1 teaspoon vanilla extract
¼ teaspoon nutmeg
¼ teaspoon cinnamon
¼ teaspoon salt

Combine all ingredients other than the blueberries in a large bowl or food processor and beat until well combined. Fold in the blueberries carefully. Grease a 12 cup muffin tin and divide the mixture between the cups. Bake in a 325 degree Fahrenheit oven for 15 to 20 minutes or until the centers have set.

*To make this recipe lower in carbohydrates, substitute your favorite no-calorie sweetener and an equivalent amount of liquid to replace the honey.

Cinnamon Roll Muffins (GF, P)

Regular cinnamon rolls rely on the gluten found in wheat flour to produce their springy texture and flaky interiors. This muffin recipe duplicates the flavors of cinnamon rolls in muffin form, but it uses no grains. You'll love the rich but healthy taste of their cinnamon topping and the moist interior of these delightful treats.

Ingredients

1 cup almond flour
¼ cup grapeseed oil
¼ cup agave nectar or maple syrup
1/8 cup coconut flour
3 eggs
1 tablespoon vanilla extract
½ teaspoon baking soda
¼ teaspoon salt
Topping
1/8 cup agave nectar or maple syrup
1 tablespoon coconut oil
1 tablespoon cinnamon

In a medium bowl, combine the flours, salt and baking soda. In a separate large bowl, blend the agave nectar or maple syrup, oil, vanilla extract and eggs. Slowly pour the dry ingredients into the wet mixture, stirring carefully until there are no lumps. Grease a 12 cup muffin tin and spoon batter into the cups. In a small bowl, blend the agave, coconut oil and cinnamon. Divide this mixture between the muffin cups and bake at 350 degrees Fahrenheit for 8 to 12 minutes or until the centers are solid.

Almond Biscuits (GF, P, LC)

These biscuits have a crisp but crumbly texture and provide plenty of protein. They're great as a part of any breakfast, but they also make an excellent addition to Thanksgiving menus, brunches, dinners and much more. To decrease the carbohydrates in this recipe, simply omit the honey.

Ingredients

2 ½ cups almond flour
2 eggs
¼ cup coconut oil
1 tablespoon honey
½ teaspoon baking soda
½ teaspoon salt

In a medium bowl, combine the almond flour, soda and salt. In a separate large bowl, blend the eggs, honey and coconut oil. Pour the dry ingredient mixture into the oil mixture, stirring continuously to produce a moldable dough. Place the dough on a piece of parchment paper and cover with an additional piece, then roll out to about 1 ½ inches in thickness. If necessary, dust the dough with additional almond flour.

Using a biscuit cutter or large mouthed glass, cut the dough into 10 biscuits, rerolling as necessary. Line a baking sheet with parchment paper. Transfer the uncooked biscuits to the sheet using a spatula and bake at 350 degrees Fahrenheit for 15 minutes, or until the bottoms of the biscuits begin to brown. Serve hot with gravy, jam or any other food.

Rye-style Flax Bread (GF, P, LC)

While a basic sandwich bread works for most uses, not every meal is appropriate for it. That's where a stronger-tasting option can help. This flax seed-based bread has the same color and general flavor as traditional rye bread, but it lacks the potentially-damaging health problems that come with that great. Eat this bread plain, toasted, or as part of your favorite sandwich. To reduce the bread's carbohydrate content, simply omit the honey or replace it with your favorite no-calorie sweetener.

Ingredients

1 cup almond flour
¾ cup ground flax seed
3 eggs
¼ cup water
2 tablespoons extra virgin olive oil
2 tablespoons caraway seeds
1 teaspoon honey
¾ teaspoon lemon juice
½ teaspoon baking soda
½ teaspoon salt
Coconut oil
Combine the ground flax seed, soda, salt and almond

flour in a large bowl. In a separate small bowl, mix the honey, water, eggs, oil and lemon juice. Slowly stir the wet ingredients into the dry mixture to form a thick batter, then add caraway seeds and mix until evenly distributed. Allow the batter to rest for 5 minutes. Grease a mini loaf pan with coconut oil and fill with the batter. Bake for 30 minutes at 350 degrees Fahrenheit, or until the center is solid. Allow the bread to cool, slice and serve.

Snacks

Homemade Yogurt (GF, P, LC*)

Whether you prefer traditional dairy yogurt or you're going milk-free, yogurt is an important staple that any grain-free cook can't do without. It's essential in many baking recipes and makes a delicious meat marinade, as well as a snack on its own. Many commercial yogurts contain large amounts of fillers, sugars and other grain-derived ingredients, making them inappropriate for all kinds of diets. Making your own allows you to control what's in your yogurt and lets you produce the perfect texture for your preferences.

Ingredients

4 cups milk, cream or coconut milk
1 tablespoon honey
1 package powdered yogurt starter

Bring the milk, coconut or cream to a boil in a large pot over high heat. Immediately remove from stove and cool to room temperature. Remove 1/2 cup of the liquid to a small separate bowl and combine with the packaged starter. Mix well, then return the starter mixture to the main bowl. Combine thoroughly and pour into a yogurt maker. Ferment for 24 to 30 hours, then remove to the refrigerator to thicken. If desired, strain the yogurt through cheesecloth suspended over a bowl to produce thicker, "Greek-style" yogurt.

*To reduce carbohydrates, omit the honey from dairy-based yogurt. This recipe relies on some sugar for successful fermentation, so no-calorie sweetener is not appropriate.

Roasted Pumpkin Seeds (GF, P, LC)

These pumpkin seeds with sweet spices are the perfect snack for the autumn holidays. Save the seeds from your jack-o-lantern or pie pumpkins to produce this simple but fragrant food. They're a great substitute for grain-based crackers and unhealthy chips.

Ingredients

½ cup fresh pumpkin seeds
1 tablespoon olive oil
½ teaspoon ginger powder
¼ teaspoon salt
¼ teaspoon allspice
¼ teaspoon cinnamon
1/8 teaspoon cardamom
1/8 teaspoon cloves
1/8 teaspoon black pepper

In a medium bowl, toss the oil with the pumpkin seeds. In a separate small bowl, combine the powdered spices and stir well. Pour over the seed mixture and stir thoroughly to coat. Bake on an ungreased cookie sheet at 375 degrees Fahrenheit or until fragrant and well-toasted. Eat while still warm or allow to cool. Store in an air-tight container.

Coconut Chicken Strips (GF, P, LC)

Coconut and chicken are a great combination, and this recipe gives you an alternative to grain-heavy fried snacking options. This baked, non-battered chicken recipe is delicious and a lot of fun to eat, whether it's as a snack or part of a special dinner. Try it with salad, guacamole, or a basic coleslaw recipe.

Ingredients

1 pound boneless, skinless chicken breasts
1 cup plain shredded coconut
½ cup coconut flour
2 eggs
1 tablespoon coconut milk
1 teaspoon garlic powder
½ teaspoon sharp paprika
salt and black pepper to taste

Flatten the chicken breasts with a mallet or rolling pin to an even thickness. Cut the meat into long pieces approximately 1 inch wide. Combine the eggs, coconut milk, salt and pepper in one small bowl. Beat vigorously until completely mixed. In a separate small bowl, mix the coconut flour, garlic powder and paprika. Place the coconut shreds in a third small bowl.

Working quickly, coat each strip first in coconut flour, then in the egg mixture. Roll the coated strips in shredded coconut and place on a large, ungreased baking sheet. Leave approximately 1 inch between strips. Bake for about 10 minutes at 400 degrees Fahrenheit, or until the chicken is cooked through completely. Eat plain or serve with homemade grain-free plum or sweet and sour sauce.

Fruit and Nut-Stuffed Pears (GF, P, LC)

Baked pears with sweet spices, rich nuts and fresh fruit is an excellent way to give yourself an energy boost without turning to crackers or cookies. This recipe is natural, healthy, and appropriate for most diets. Very low-carb dieters may find the sugars in the fruit to be excessive, but most should be able to eliminate the honey and still enjoy this treat.

Ingredients

4 fat, flat-bottomed pears
¼ pound red grapes
¼ cup natural apple juice
2 tablespoons honey
½ cup sliced almonds
½ lemon
1 teaspoon cinnamon

In a small bowl, combine 1 tablespoon of honey with the sliced almonds. Line a baking sheet or pie plate with parchment paper. Bake the almonds on top of the parchment at 300 degrees Fahrenheit for 15 or 20 minutes, or until crisp. Core the pears from the top, leaving the bottom solid. Place the pears on a separate pie plate, cored ends up. Dice the grapes and place them in a small bow. Combine the almond mixture with the grapes and stuff the pears. Juice the lemon and combine it with the apple juice, remaining honey and cinnamon in a small bowl. Pour this mixture into the stuffed cores and all around each piece of fruit. Bake at 300 degrees Fahrenheit for 30 minutes, or until the pears are tender and fully-cooked.

Sesame Almond Crackers (GF, P, LC)

Chips and crackers make for appealing snacking, but their high percentage of grains and other unhealthy carbohydrates can be damaging to your body. That's why these buttery or coconut-flavored seed-based crackers are such a good alternative. You'll get that savory, crunchy experience you've been craving without the grain.

Ingredients

¾ cup almond flour
2 tablespoons butter or coconut oil
1 egg white
1 tablespoon sesame seeds
3/8 teaspoon salt
¼ teaspoon onion powder
¼ teaspoon garlic powder

Beat the egg white until frothy. Allow the butter to soften at room temperature. In a small bowl, combine all dry ingredients, then blend in egg white and butter until a soft dough forms. Chill for 30 minutes, then drop by ¼ teaspoons onto a baking sheet lined with parchment. Leave 1 inch or more between dough balls. Cover with parchment paper or plastic wrap and flatten to about 1/16 inch thick. Prick with a fork and bake for 20 minutes at 325 degrees Fahrenheit, or until golden brown. Allow to cool and store in an airtight container.

Cheese Crisps (GF, P*, LC)

Crispy, crunchy and composed entirely of cheese, these unique little snacks are a grain-free dieter's snacking salvation. They're low in carbohydrates and high in flavor, making them a satisfying choice for between-meal treats. Try several different kinds of cheese to make a variety mix. Plus, these simple crisps can be made in the microwave!

Ingredients

8 ounce bag shredded cheddar, mozzarella, Swiss or Monterey jack cheese
garlic powder or onion powder to taste (optional)

Line a microwaveable plate or tray with parchment paper. Place 1 tablespoon of shredded cheese in the middle of the plate and spread it out into an even layer approximately 3 inches across. Microwave on high for 30 seconds. Remove the paper and crisp from the plate and allow it to cool, then peel the paper off of the crisp. Repeat using the same piece of parchment paper. When all crisps are cool, store in an air-tight container. For longer storage, try the freezer.

*Paleo dieters may need to eat these in moderation, as

some diets restrict dairy.

Chicken Cracklings (GF, P, LC)

These meaty snacks may sound a little unusual at first, but they'll soon grow on you. They're made using the same theory as pork rinds, but without the pig. The result is salty, meaty and surprisingly low in "bad" fats. This recipe is also great for using the skin from chicken thigh recipes that require skinless meat.

Ingredients

Skin from 8 pre-roasted chicken thighs
Salt and pepper to taste

Cut the pieces of skin into pieces a few inches across and spread them in a single layer on a large baking sheet. Avoid stacking the skins, as this can prevent crisping. Season lightly with salt on one side and bake for 30 minutes at 350 degrees Fahrenheit. Flip the skin and bake an additional 10 minutes, or until crisp and brown. Eat immediately or allow the cracklings to cool and store in the refrigerator. Reheat before serving.

Salads, Soups and Sides

Creamy Cauliflower Soup (GF, P, LC)

This rich and delicious soup makes a great substitute for potato or grain-based soups on a chilly day. It's also egg free, for diets that limit egg consumption. Substitute vegetable stock for the chicken stock to make this dish vegetarian-friendly for larger gatherings or guests.

1 head cauliflower
2 quarts chicken stock
1 large onion
¼ cup milk
2 tablespoons olive oil
1 teaspoons them
salt and pepper to taste

Chop the onion and the cauliflower. Mince the garlic. Heat the olive oil in a large pot over medium heat and sauté the onion and garlic for 5 minutes, or until translucent. Add the stock, thyme and cauliflower, then bring to a boil over high heat. Reduce to a simmer and cook until the cauliflower almost dissolves. Puree in a blender until completely smooth, then season with salt and pepper as desired. Serve hot, garnished with thyme.

Matzoh Ball Soup (GF, P, LC)

This traditional Passover soup is also beloved by plenty of non-Jewish cooks. It's known as a health-boosting remedy for cold or flu, but the wheat-based matzoh it requires is off-limits for grain-free diets. This version uses almond flour instead of wheat flour to produce surprisingly authentic-tasting matzoh balls. Whether you'd like a wheat-free substitute for your Passover table or you just love chicken soup, this recipe will soon be staple of your cookbook. To render the soup vegetarian-friendly, simply substitute vegetable broth instead of chicken.

Ingredients

6 cups chicken stock
2 cups almond flour
4 eggs
2 teaspoons salt
pepper to taste

Combine eggs, salt and pepper in a medium bowl, beating vigorously. Slowly add the almond flour, stirring continuously to produce a soft dough. Refrigerate for at least 2 hours and set aside. Boil a large pot of water over high heat and drop the batter by tablespoons-full into the boiling liquid. Reduce heat to low, cover, and allow to simmer for 20 minutes. Remove with a slotted spoon. In a separate pot, heat 6 cups chicken stock to a simmer. Gently place the finished matzoh balls into the stock and heat for an additional 10 minutes. Serve hot, with at least 2 to 3 matzoh balls per bowl.

Split Pea and Mushroom Soup (GF)

This hearty soup provides protein in the form of mushrooms and split peas, savory flavors from stock, garlic and onion, and a little spice in the form of paprika. This recipe contains no meat, but if you'd like more of a meaty flavor, substitute chicken or beef stock for the vegetable broth. Like many hearty soups, this recipe is actually best the next day.

Ingredients

1 quart vegetable broth
3 cups water
1 cup split yellow peas
½ pound mushrooms
1 cup kale
2 tablespoons olive oil
2 cloves garlic
1 small onion
2 bay leaves
½ teaspoon smoked paprika
salt and black pepper to taste

Combine bay leaves, split peas, water and paprika in a medium pan. Bring to a boil over high heat, then reduce to low and simmer until the peas fall apart. Remove from heat and set aside. Discard bay leaves. Chop onions, kale and garlic. In a large pan, heat the olive oil to medium-low and sauté chopped onion. Slice the mushrooms and add to the pan with the garlic and kale. Cook until tender and set aside. Remove bay leaf from split peas. Combine pea mixture with mushroom mixture along with stock. Cook for 30 minutes or until thick and well combined. Serve hot.

Squash Oven Fries (GF, P, LC)

Even for potato eaters, conventional fries tend to be off-limits for a grain-free diet because of the risk that they have been cooked in corn oil. These lower-carbohydrate substitutes are made from squash, cooked in olive oil, and made right in your home oven. They're crisp and much healthier. Choose them as a side for your next batch of barbecue chicken or even to go with your morning eggs.

Ingredients

1 large butternut squash or pumpkin
¼ cup olive oil
1 tablespoon dried oregano
salt and black pepper to taste

Cut the squash in half lengthwise and remove the seeds. Peel the outside and cut the meat into sticks of your preferred size. Place the squash fries in a large bowl and toss them with the olive oil, then the spices. Season to taste with salt and pepper. Place in a single layer on a large cookie sheet and roast at 425 degrees Fahrenheit for 20 minutes, or until the outside is crisp.

Cranberry Steak Salad (GF, P, LC)

This salad is hearty enough to be a meal in and of itself. It uses skirt steak, which is not normally considered a tender or appealing cut, but careful preparation helps bring out the incredible flavors of this meat. When combined with fresh cranberries and fennel, it produces a fresh salad that's affordable and delicious. If fresh cranberries are unavailable in your area, consider substituting frozen.

1 pound skirt steak
2 cups arugula
1 large bulb fennel
½ cup fresh cranberries
2 scallions
1 tablespoon olive oil
1 tablespoon fresh thyme
1 tablespoon fresh basil
1 bunch flat leaf parsley
salt and pepper to taste
3 tablespoons of your favorite vinaigrette

Fill a small pot with water and bring it to a boil over high heat. Add the cranberries and cook for about 5 minutes, or until the berries soften. Drain and set aside to cool. Season the steak with salt and black pepper to taste, then sprinkle thoroughly with basil and thyme. Heat the coconut oil in a large skillet over medium-high heat and add the steak. Cook, flipping frequently throughout the process, until the steak reaches your preferred level of doneness. Transfer to a plate or cutting board and allow to rest for 5 minutes.

Slice the fennel thinly and combine in a large bowl with the cranberries and arugula. Cut the steak into thin slices and toss with the vegetables. Serve topped with your favorite dressing and garnish with parsley.

Spinach and Blood Orange Salad (GF, P)

Light and refreshing, this salad is a delicious starter or small meal. The fruit adds tartness and sweetness, while the spinach provides plenty of important minerals. Combined with honey and almonds, this recipe is a great meatless addition to just about any meal. If you can't obtain blood oranges, consider substituting Meyer lemons or sweet pink grapefruit.

Ingredients

½ cup spinach leaves
2 medium blood oranges
1 sweet pear
½ cup slivered or chopped almonds
¼ cup dried, unsweetened cranberries
1 tablespoon honey
Dressing
½ cup olive oil
2 tablespoons rice vinegar
1 teaspoon prepared brown mustard
salt and pepper to taste

In a small bowl, combine the honey with the almonds. Line a baking sheet with parchment paper and spread the almonds over it. Bake at 300 degrees Fahrenheit for

15 to 20 minutes or until browned. Remove and set aside.

In a separate bowl, combine the olive oil, rice vinegar, mustard, salt and pepper. Whisk vigorously to combine and set aside. Cut the pear and citrus fruit into large pieces. Combine in a large bowl with the spinach and dried cranberries. Pour the vinaigrette over the entire salad and toss. Serve garnished with honeyed almonds.

Kale Coleslaw (GF, P, LC)

Traditional cabbage coleslaw is perfectly appropriate for a grain-free diet, as long as you can ensure that the dressing includes no dextrose or other grain-derived ingredients. This recipe provides a little extra punch, however. It includes nutrient-dense kale and almonds, making it much healthier than the standard fare.

Ingredients

2 large bunches kale
1 pound carrots
2 scallions
½ cup olive oil
½ cup coconut oil
¼ cup chopped almonds
2 egg yolks
1 tablespoon lemon juice
1 tablespoon prepared mustard
salt and pepper to taste

Cut the kale and scallions into thin strips. Shred the carrots and toss with the kale mixture. Mix in the almonds, stirring carefully. Mix the olive and coconut oils together in a small pan or microwaveable bowl and heat until just melted. In a small bowl, combine the egg yolks, mustard and 1 teaspoon of the lemon juice. Whisk vigorously, dripping the melted oils in slowly to create an emulsion. Stabilize the bowl with a cloth or towel if necessary. When the dressing reaches the desired consistency, add the remaining lemon juice. Season with salt and pepper. Add 2 or 3 tablespoons of dressing to the kale mixture and stir to coat. Refrigerate and serve cold.

Roasted Winter Squash (GF, P, LC)

This simple side dish is tasty and appropriate for a wide range of diet restrictions. It's gluten-free, contains no dairy, and also lacks meat. Some low-carbohydrate diets prohibit winter squash, but this mildly-sweet dish should be appropriate for the later stages of these eating plans. Enjoy roasted squash as a side with your favorite meats or on its own as a light meal.

Ingredients

1 acorn squash or 2 delicata squash
¼ cup olive or coconut oil
1 teaspoon cinnamon
salt and pepper to taste

Cut the squash in half lengthwise and remove the stems, seeds and membranes. Place cut side down on a cutting board and cut into slices about ¼ inch thick. Lay in a single layer on a large cookie sheet, leaving space between each piece. Drizzle with 1/8 cup oil, then sprinkle with salt, pepper and cinnamon. Bake at 400 degrees Fahrenheit for 10 minutes, or until golden brown. Flip, drizzle with the remaining oil, and bake for an additional 5 minutes. Serve hot.

5-Day Grain Free Meal Plan

This sample grain free meal plan is designed to help you get an idea of the best way to go grain free. It is not oriented toward any one type of diet, however. That means that if you need to avoid specific ingredients, it may be necessary to modify the meal plan slightly. Use this diet plan as a springboard for your new way of cooking, rather than an exact set of rules. After all, there's nothing to limit you other than your imagination!

Day 1

Breakfast: Hot Porridge, orange juice

Lunch: Cranberry Steak Salad

Snack: Cheese Crisps, sliced pears

Dinner: Braised Chicken with Sweet Potatoes and Fennel Bulb, Spinach and Blood Orange Salad

Day 2

Breakfast: Green Eggs, Rye-style Flax Bread

Lunch: Split Pea and Mushroom Soup

Snack: Homemade Yogurt

Dinner: Stuffed Bell Peppers with Veal, Kale Coleslaw

Day 3

Breakfast: Banana Coconut Muffins

Lunch: American Taco Pie

Snack: Cinnamon Roll Muffins

Dinner: Pot Roast with Fresh Vegetables, Almond Biscuits

Day 4

Breakfast: Sweet Potato Breakfast Casserole

Lunch: Roasted Winter Squash, Coconut Chicken Strips

Snack: Fruit and Nut-Stuffed Pears

Dinner: Creamy Cauliflower Soup, Barbecue Chicken with Grain-free Sauce

Day 5

Breakfast: Almond Waffles, orange juice, Homemade Yogurt

Lunch: Baked Cashew Chicken

Snack: Roasted Pumpkin Seeds

Dinner: Zucchini Pasta with Roasted Sweet Potatoes and Coconut Pesto, Squash Oven Fries, Coconut-vanilla Frozen Dessert

Conclusion

There's no reason to feel like eating grain-free has to be a limitation. The world is full of fantastic and healthy grain-free recipes that are suitable for paleo dieters, celiacs and other with wheat sensitivities, and low-carb eating plans. If you just take a little bit of time to think about all the options, you'll be surprised by all the great things you can eat. While it can be difficult living in a wheat and corn-obsessed world, you won't be in danger of going hungry. All you have to do with learn to think outside the grain-based box.

These recipes provide a starting place for anyone who wants to enjoy their food without worrying about the health problems that grains and other carbohydrates could be causing. It's time to stop suffering from headaches, digestive problems, nutritional deficiencies and all the other issues that modern grains can induce. The alternatives are rich, delicious and extremely healthy. Try a new no-grain recipe today!